WARNING

This book may be extremely dangerous to the life expectancy of a poor, tired, anemic worklife.

ABOUT TOM JACKSON

Over the past ten years, Tom Jackson has emerged as one of the nation's leading authorities and commentators on the nature and quality of people's worklives. His place is at the cutting edge of a revolutionary new approach to the way people deal with their careers.

Jackson's work takes him deeply into the corporate world of human resources management, and career development, as well as to the very pragmatic realities of thousands of individual job seekers and career changers each year in workshops and courses he and his staff conduct.

Recent books by Jackson are *Hidden Job Market, 28 Days to a Better Job, Guerrilla Tactics in the Job Market.* He is also the creator of over one dozen other training programs and materials in the area of employment and manpower, used by corporations, schools and individuals.

He is President of The Career Development Team, Inc. in New York City, and Employment Training Corporation.

The Perfect Resume

Tom Jackson

AN ANCHOR PRESS BOOK
DOUBLEDAY
NEW YORK   LONDON   TORONTO   SYDNEY   AUCKLAND

AN ANCHOR PRESS BOOK
Published by Doubleday, a division of Bantam Doubleday Dell Publishing Group, Inc., 666 Fifth Avenue, New York, New York 10103.

ANCHOR PRESS, DOUBLEDAY and the portrayal of an anchor are trademarks of Doubleday, a division of Bantam Doubleday Dell Publishing Group, Inc.

This book is dedicated to a purpose: *To expand people's ability to come from who they are into the work world, in a way that produces satisfaction and aliveness for them, and value for others.*

Contents

To Write a Book on Resumes . . .

Find someone like Ellen Perry—a top professional career developer and counselor—who is willing to spend hundreds of hours, often deep into the night, to sort through thousands of sample resumes, selecting, editing, revising, and clarifying.

Add an Audrey Hagemaier who has the dedication to clear layout and design, and commitment to quality of communication, which is essential to this type of work.

Bring in Kevin Lane for late night typing, editing, and retyping from the author's inexcusable illegibility.

Be sure to have someone like Ruth Gutstein to supervise and manage the accurate assembly and continuity of the final project.

Don't forget to have a personal editor of the intelligence and commitment of Judy Oringer to ensure clarity, consistency, and consciousness.

And don't even start the project unless you can find a publisher like Doubleday, and an editor like Loretta Barrett to recognize and support (and demand) the best that you can achieve.

This book is a product of our combined commitment to you, the reader.

Tom Jackson
New York City, 1980

How to Use This Book

This book is a resource for you and has been designed to be *used* and not just *read* and digested. Its purpose is to assist you in putting together the best possible personal statement of your skills, abilities, and accomplishments, in a way that will motivate employers to want to see you and to want to discuss employment possibilities.

Depending upon where you stand in your career—how much you have already done to prepare yourself—you will need or want to use different parts of the book to write a perfect resume for yourself. Shown below are three alternative ways to get the best from this volume.

THE VERY SHORT COURSE

If you are already very *clear about your job target* or work direction and have had *good prior experience with resumes,* and feel confident in *your writing skills,* you can effectively prepare your resume by hitting the following key stepping-stones in the book. This will save you hours.

1. Remind yourself of the underlying principles of an effective resume. Read Inside the Executive Suite, pages 9–13.

2. Read pages 50–59 about job targeting and fill in the information on page 60.

3. Select the best resume format that best represents you after reading pages 65–71.

4. Use the appropriate resume drafting forms for the format you have chosen. See pages 85–127 for directions.

5. Review the appropriate resume samples. See the Index to Sample Resumes on pages 149–153.

6. Perfect your resume in Step 5, pages 128–132.

7. Put together a perfect cover letter with the information on pages 133–137.

8. Brush up on job hunting skills, pages 205–208.
   (Note: *And don't forget you can go over any other parts of the book you wish, to stress what you already know.*)

THE SHORT COURSE

If you are very certain about your job target or work direction but not certain about how to effectively represent that in your resume, follow this simple path:

1. Discover the underlying principles of

the perfect resume by reading Inside the Executive Suite, pages 9–13.

2. Read pages 50–59 about job targeting and fill in your targets on page 60.

3. Read and do all of Section 3, Preparing the Perfect Resume, pages 65–84.

4. Review the appropriate sample resumes. See the Resume Selector on pages 149–153 .

5. Prepare a perfect cover letter, pages 133–137.

6. Brush up on your job hunting skills, pages 205–208.

THE FULL COURSE

If you are ready and willing to take a fresh look at your work direction, or if the idea of having a specific job target that represents both your skills and interests intrigues you, and you also are interested in having the fullest possible support in preparing the perfect resume for yourself, you are in exactly the right place at the right time—this entire book is for you.

Find yourself a comfortable place in which to work. Get out the pencils and paper. Heat up the coffeepot. Start the process from the beginning and work your way through to the perfect resume ending. And as a bonus, go over the job-finding tips at the back of the book.

THE CAREER DISCOVERY PROCESS

We are very proud to be able to include in this book a completely separate section designed to assist in one of the most difficult tasks that most people ever face in their worklives: selection of a satisfying work direction or job target.

This process, which is the culmination of many years' development, with literally thousands of individual and group counseling sessions and workshops, is designed to penetrate beyond the superficial vocational aptitude approach, into a deeper realm of personal awareness and self-understanding, in a way that can be translated into the pragmatic reality of today's work world.

You do not *need* to do this process in order to create a perfect resume, although we know that you will find it to be a valuable and expanding exercise.

AND MORE . . .

In the closing pages we have included a distillation of some valuable job-finding tips that will help speed you, perfect resume in hand, into the job targets of your choice.

Happy hunting—and cheers!

Preliminaries

INSIDE THE EXECUTIVE SUITE

Consider this: Roger Dupré, the employment manager of Aspect Publishing, a Midwestern firm specializing in sales promotional materials, has had a rotten day. He started out late due to a flat tire discovered just as he was about to head for the office. Frustration mounted when he got to work and found his parking place taken by a visitor, and had to circle the lot twice and park three blocks away.

That was just the beginning—things continued downhill. Two unexpected meetings, a dozen or so unavoidable phone calls, materials delivered late from the printers, an angry manager with a labor grievance that needed to be handled.

And, to top it all, a visit from his boss late in the day complaining that the computer department still hadn't seen any applicants for their three new job openings.

Roger held his breath and counted to ten when his boss left, lowering his blood pressure a few points and allowing his mind to ease back from red alert. He had

been here before, and knew that there was no easy way around the problems. He buzzed his secretary: "Phyllis, it's another one of those days, I'm afraid, except worse. Pat was down asking about those computer openings we got last week—she'd had a complaint from the department because they haven't seen anyone yet. I don't know why they're complaining so soon, we just got the openings, didn't we?"

"Well, not exactly," she replied, "we actually got the orders two weeks ago. We've run an ad in the *Trib,* and alerted the agencies."

"But what's happened—have we gotten any response? I haven't seen anything."

"Oh yes," she replied. "We've had an enormous response. From our ad alone we've gotten over a hundred resumes, and dozens more from the agencies. They're still coming in. You told me to hold onto the responses, and you would go over them when things calmed down and you had some time. I probably should have reminded you but you've been so busy. I'm sorry."

Roger didn't know whether to laugh or

cry. On the one hand, it was good to know that there was something to work with on the openings. On the other hand, he shuddered at the thought of going through all those resumes. No wonder he had conveniently forgotten about the openings.

"Okay, Phyllis—do me a favor, put them all in a box. I'll take them home and go over them tonight when I have at least a little peace and quiet. Next time, don't let me put this stuff off."

Later that night, with the kid in bed, his late supper downed—digestion stimulated by two martinis and a cigar—Roger sets out to review the aspirations and careers of 152 job candidates for three positions. The task is formidable: every resume and every letter is different—from one-page handwritten notes, to a twelve-page "personal presentation."

Most of what he reads is irrelevant and poorly organized. Long sentences and paragraphs without pause or punctuation. Some, just bare-bones outlines of job titles spanning dozens of years of work, but without a hint of accomplishment, or results produced. Roger's mind goes on automatic, his analytical judgment is short-circuited by the very difficult task of simply reading the information, let alone relating it to his company's needs. Document by document, he sorts the papers into two stacks: *Consider Further* and *Reject*—the basic geometry of the employment-screening process. Later, he will take the *Consider Further* pile and sort through these resumes again. Then again, each time rejecting those that don't grab his attention. Despite his promise to himself to look through the rejects again, he won't get around to them, and in a week or so their authors will all get polite turndown letters.

Roger has fallen into a pattern—perhaps unconsciously—a pattern that is repeated every single day by thousands of employers involved in the screening process. Without being aware of it, and faced with a virtually impossible amount of raw, unorganized, non-standard data—resumes of every possible type and description, he has opted for the now standard initial screening process, which has become largely the measurement not of the abilities and accomplishments of the candidates, but the quality of the resumes themselves.

To restate this: To allow employers to face the necessity of having to read a large volume of non-standard resumes, the initial screening cycles end up being based not upon the inherent qualities of the candidate, but upon the quality and clarity of the resumes. Another way to say it: Well-qualified people are frequently not considered for good positions because of poor resumes. And the opposite: Less qualified persons will greatly improve their chances to get interviews and offers by developing good resumes.

Marshall McLuhan said it more concisely: "The Medium is the Message."

WHAT IS THE PERFECT RESUME?

The perfect resume is a written communication that clearly demonstrates your ability to produce results in an area of concern to potential employers, in a way that motivates them to meet you.

Be willing to analyze that description with us further, as it reflects the basic philosophy of this book. The key concepts:

COMMUNICATION

The essential ingredient in communication, from our point of view, is personal responsibility. The definition we use is this: *Real communication is being respon-*

sible (100 percent) to ensure that a message is received. This means that if the reader doesn't get it you didn't communicate. As simple as that. You don't get to blame the other guy. Habitually, most of us approach non-communication by blaming someone else. "He never listens to me." "They're too dumb to understand this." "They never told me." These are common responses to the non-communicative environment in which we live. They deny our responsibility in the matter.

The excitement of being responsible for your communication creates a livelier game. You get to look at ways to improve your effectiveness. You attract constructive criticism and use it to improve. You get to be more powerful and able, and people know it. In using this book, you are exercising responsibility for the effectiveness of your resume.

CLEARLY DEMONSTRATE

The resume does more than describe. By the way it is put together it actually *shows* the reader how you do things. At one level it demonstrates how well you have mastered written communication—a key part of almost every valuable job these days.

At another level, the resume is a personal presentation of how well you think of yourself. It is almost an axiom in career counseling that what an employer thinks of you ends up being pretty close to what *you* think of you. The resume demonstrates your self-appraisal.

At a final level, the resume, like your job campaign itself, demonstrates how you will get the job done. Your resume can be seen as a work project that you take on with yourself as the employer. How well you got the job done is available for all to see.

ABILITY TO PRODUCE RESULTS

At the bottom line, *results* are all that employers want. Not reasons, not explanations, not hopes, not excuses. Not even, for that matter, experience or education, although employers use these as predictors. *Results.* What happened when you arrived? What was produced or what could *we* produce with you on our team? In a fast-moving, technologically oriented work world, yesterday's education and job may be irrelevant to the new problems that need to be faced. The resume is not your biography. *It is a prospectus for the future.*

CONCERN TO POTENTIAL EMPLOYERS

The resume is not the whole story. It is a directed communication to a particular audience: employers whom you have selected as meeting *your* qualifications.

Yes, we see *you* in the driver's seat in your career. You select job targets that represent the marriage of your own essential life interests and skills—and come *from* these job targets into the work world. The resume is designed to communicate specifically to that audience and to no other. If you have three job targets, you will have three different resumes.

MOTIVATED TO MEET YOU PERSONALLY

The resume is not designed to get you the position. Sorry, but that's a fact of job life. The best that your resume will do for you is to get you interviews and add some points on the scale for the final consideration. Employers don't hire on the basis of a resume alone, except in situations that are too rare to be included here.

A good interview is an important necessity following the resume (see pages 206–207 for some interviewing tips).

But the perfect resume *will get you interviews,* and with employers who count. By demonstrating that you have a valuable, potential contribution to make, you move the job search process to the next major level . . .

And a dividend. The purpose of the resume, as we discussed above, is to get you interviews with employers who meet your job target criteria. But there is another payoff, and that is to help you focus consciously on yourself and your worklife. To get in touch with where you are and where you want to go with your work. The very process of going through the material in this book will assist you to improve the quality of your worklife and, therefore, the quality of your life, since both are inextricably related.

THE RULES OF THE GAME

Someone invites you over for a friendly game of cards, or backgammon, or football, or quoits. You accept. And when you turn the first card or roll the dice, or put the ball in play, one thing is probably a certainty. You and your co-players are all basically on the same wavelength about the ways the game is played. If not, you don't play. You wouldn't put a dollar down on a poker table unless you knew the rules. To do otherwise would brand you as a "sucker," in the impolite parlance of cardsharps.

All games have rules. The job game has rules. When you know the rules, you take away much of the confusion, mystery, and surprise.

This book is about the rules for resumes. It is also a book about winning strategies. Please don't put the biggest stakes you've got—your worklife—into the pot unless you know the rules of the game.

WHO NEEDS IT?

Probably you. Years ago, resumes were assembled primarily by people of distinctly professional class—educators, lawyers, professional managers, and the like. Today, with increased specialization and mobility, the use of resumes extends through all white-collar levels from executive to hourly worker—in lower-paying blue-collar and unskilled occupations. The test for using or not using a resume is whether a person would typically show up for an interview, get hired, and start work the same day, or become involved in a longer hiring procedure in which the resume would precede or follow the interview.

Regardless of level or scope of your work targets, a resume can't hurt. By putting yourself through the discipline of preparing the perfect resume, you will have greater clarity about your work life purpose and will increase your ability to present yourself in a way that motivates employers.

And it takes some work for you to do it. Which brings us to:

THE PAYOFF FOR YOU

The easy way to prepare a resume is to sit down at a typewriter or pad of paper, start at the upper left-hand corner of the page, type or write down the facts and information as they occur to you, until you get to the lower right, make a few corrections, have it retyped if necessary, and then crank out fifty copies or so on the local photocopy machine, put them in the mail, and then sit back and wait . . .

and wait . . . and wait. Time to prepare: perhaps three hours. Time to wait for the right response: six to eight weeks—or longer.

In this book we have laid out a tougher path for you to follow. We have designed an approach that will move you out of novice class and on toward the higher rank of career professional.

Most of the book calls for your direct participation. By going through the perfect resume process we've outlined, you will have a resume equal to those of the top 10 percent of all job seekers. The cost to you in preparation time is perhaps twenty to thirty hours. The payoff can be immense—three or four times the response from the employers *you* are interested in, and a more powerful selling tool in the bargain.

In cold hard cash alone, the value of a perfect resume is probably an additional 10 percent in your paycheck, due to the increased value of yourself that you have communicated.

In terms of increased potential for personal satisfaction in your work, the rewards are priceless. Hundreds of people who have used these procedures, have clarified their own interests and abilities and have learned how to prepare the best resumes, have enabled themselves to cre-ate their own job directions and achieved them. They have blazed a trail for you to follow. But watch out—there are pitfalls and personal barriers that can get in the way.

PITFALLS AND PERSONAL BARRIERS

Fifteen years of working with people in their job campaigns has taught us one very important lesson, which in our work has come to be called *The rule of inherent negativity*. It can be stated like this: *People very frequently do not operate in their own best interests.* We know, in advance, that there will be many temptations for you not to follow the detailed steps outlined in this book *even though you believe them to be valuable for you.*

You may find yourself impatiently short-cutting from an earlier page in the book to a spot further along. This is a natural reaction to a subject that is as personal and introspective as creating a resume that really touches who you are. Please be prepared for the temptation to skip ahead, and know that your fertile mind will probably come up with a few excuses or reasons to explain or justify these jumps. See how many of these excuses you can identify in advance on the following checklist:

EXCUSES CHECKLIST

Check any of the statements below that you feel might be used by you as reasons (real or imagined) or excuses to stop you from following the perfect resume process, which will be presented in this book:

_____ I don't have enough time to do all the preliminary stuff. I want a resume right away.

_____ I don't need to even look at my job targets. I already know exactly what I want to do.

_____ Writing a resume is easy. This book complicates it.

_____ This book is not for people at my level—it's for those who are more qualified.

_____ This book is not for people at my level—it's for those who are less qualified.

_____ My old resume is good enough for me—after all, it has worked before.

_____ I don't need a resume since I've never had any formal work experience.

_____ It's too complicated for me.

_____ It's too simple for me.

_____ I don't like a book that argues with me.

_____ Why bother, there are no satisfying jobs for me out there anyway.

_____ I'm too old.

_____ I'm too young.

_____ I'm too lazy for this sort of thing.

_____ (You fill in)   _____

_____ (You fill in)   _____

However or whatever you answered above—or even if you didn't answer—*thank you* for being with us so far and for participating in the perfect resume process. You may use as much or as little of this text as you care to or as, in your judgment, you find valuable. We aren't stuck on your doing all of it, and we *do* want you to give it a try.

TEN MOST COMMON RESUME WRITING MISTAKES

We've surveyed scores of prime employers, career counselors, and employment agencies to determine what they feel are the most common repeated mistakes in the thousands of resumes they see. Here are the top (bottom) ten:

1. Too long (preferred length is one page).
2. Disorganized—information is scattered around the page—hard to follow.
3. Poorly typed and printed—hard to read—looks unprofessional.
4. Overwritten—long paragraphs and sentences—takes too long to say too little.
5. Too sparse—gives only bare essentials of dates and job titles.
6. Not oriented for results—doesn't show what the candidate accomplished on the job.
7. Too many irrelevancies—height, weight, sex, health, marital status are not needed on today's resumes.
8. Misspellings, typographical errors, poor grammar—resumes should be carefully proofread before they are printed and mailed.
9. Tries too hard—fancy typesetting and binders, photographs and exotic paper stocks distract from the clarity of the presentation.
10. Misdirected—too many resumes arrive on employers' desks unrequested, and with little or no apparent connections to the organization—cover letters would help avoid this.

On the following page is a fairly typical resume of a job candidate who came to one of our workshops (all names and addresses have been changed in this book to protect the innocent—and the guilty!). On the facing page is the resume produced after going through our processes.

BEFORE

CONFIDENTIAl

R E S U M E

Name: Daniel Hartman   Age: 46
Address: 3416 Halub Avenue   Height: 5' 10"
          Philadelphia, Pennsylvania 18042   Weight: 200
Phone: (215) 246-5818   Marital Status:
                                                    Married, 4 sons
                                                Health: Good

JOB OBJECTIVE: Position as Coordinator in Manufacturing or
                 Packaging Equipment

EMPLOYMENT:

1975 to Present   Present position is technical writer of instruc-
United Pkg. Co.   tion books, catalogs and illustrations in Machine
                  Design.

1963 to 1975   Packaging System and Sales where I was in charge
United Pkg. Co.   of a small shop and Parts Department on overhauling
                  equipment and change parts to ship to customers.
                  I did various accounting functions such as
                  monthly income statement, inventory control
                  and billing. I also kept cost of engineering
                  design projects.

1955 to 1963   Production Planning Department (soap).
United Pkg. Co.   Scheduling various departments and also ordering
                  raw materials.

EDUCATION:

Wilson High School (Academic-Vocational) 1949
Inter Plant Courses - 1956 to 1960
Electrical, Heat seal, Tool & Die Design, Pulp & Paper
Southampton County Community College - Accounting I & II
Introduction to Data Processing Seminars
Indistrial Management
Technical Writing

AFTER

Daniel Hartman
3416 Halub Avenue
Philadelphia, Pennsylvania   18042
(215) 246-5818

* WORK EXPERIENCE *

UNITED PACKAGING COMPANY
1955 to Present

COORDINATOR
FIELD ENGINEERING: Coordinated manufacturing and packaging equipment.
                        Managed records of all engineering projects - hours,
                        material, and total costs. Handled inventory
                        control of machine parts and equipment. Completely
                        coordinated monthly income statement of department.
                        Managed three machinists in work load schedule.

TECHNICAL WRITER: Coordinated technical information from engineers.
                        Organized instruction books, catalogs, and brochures.
                        Handled coloring, labeling, illustrations, and minor
                        technical writing. Coordinated photography, making
                        of progress report charts, and transparencies for
                        overhead projection and book revisions.

PRODUCTION PLANNER: Scheduled machines to work efficiently. Handled
                        inventory control of various raw materials - boxes
                        and cartons.

* EDUCATION *

Southampton County Community College - Accounting & Data Processing

Inter-plant Courses - Electrical, heat seal, tool and die design, pulp
                      and paper

Industrial Management and technical writing courses

THE CAREER DISCOVERY PROCESS

Years ago, when we first started to read and critique resumes for people, we kept running into a problem: the resume was not focused toward a particular job target or goal and, as a result, wandered rather aimlessly around the person's skills and abilities with little direction or clarity.

We discovered that, with a majority of clients, to start to assist with the resume was like picking up a problem in the middle. We didn't have enough information to really help the job seeker present himself or herself in the proper focus. Hours would be required to answer that persistent job seeker's lament: "I don't know what I want to do."

Over the succeeding dozen years of working on the front lines of the job search, we have devised and tested an evolving set of approaches to assist people in the discovery and definition of their career goals and job targets, which are,

of course, followed by hard-hitting resumes that support and promote these goals.

In the next two chapters we have presented for your use our current version of a personal process that you can use to discover and reinforce your own career goals.

The Career Discovery Process is an important process and is not required if you are already very certain about your job targets and your skills and interests. If you want to move right into the resume preparation, you can skip to page 63 and go to work.

On the other hand, if you would like to explore, or re-explore, your basic skills and abilities and see how they fit into a satisfying job direction for you, we invite you to participate in the Career Discovery Process.

Defining Your Magnificence

"The problem with most resumes is not so much the form of them, although that's bad enough, it's deeper than that. It's that the people who write them aren't really in touch with who they are—what they have to offer. Their magnificence, if you will. And it shows. Tell them not to rush into the resume right away. To sit back and take inventory first."

Employment manager of one of the nation's largest blue-chip corporations

Yes, magnificence. Notice the resistance and doubt that surge forward at even the simple thought: Who me, magnificent?

The answer is yes, you. In your own particular configuration of skills, abilities, aptitudes, interests, energy, dedication, inspiration, and willingness to make a contribution, you are unique. Special. And perhaps you aren't in touch with that. Most of us aren't. It's much more common for people to be in touch with their insignificance, to have a ready reference of the things they can't do as well as someone else, to be controlled by their shortcomings. People invalidate themselves for what they aren't rather than for what they really are.

Magnificence doesn't have a particular shape or form. It doesn't require outside approval or agreement. All it takes is the willingness to get in touch with what you do have, rather than what you don't have—who you are, not who you aren't. And then, to present this to the world with pride and certainty rather than apology and equivocation.

Here in the Career Discovery Process, we are going to assist you to get in touch with the basic qualities and components out of which to fashion your perfect resume—to uncover the primary sales points that will enhance your presentation to potential employers. We intend, in the process, for you to go beyond your own immediate self-image and to get in touch with the value and significance to others of some things about yourself that you have probably taken for granted.

As most career counselors, psychologists, and employment experts will agree, self-analysis is one of the hardest things people have to face in organizing their job searches. The Career Discovery Process will make the task easier, and perhaps even enjoyable.

YOU ARE NOT YOUR JOB TITLE (OR MAJOR FIELD OF STUDY)

If you have been working or going to school for a few years, by this time in your life you and the world have probably reached an agreement about what you are. You have, undoubtedly, temporarily satisfied the search for identity by assuming a work title. After years of study you can now call yourself an engineer, or account executive or executive secretary, or steelworker or teacher, or career counselor. In short, you have pigeonholed yourself. And it's comfortable.

The problem is that this approach to your work life doesn't really support you very much. Every year, in our corporate career development work, we deal with men and women who have resigned themselves to their job titles, and surrendered to their identities rather than create them. We work with people who have lost touch with what they can do outside their job duties. People who feel stuck with a narrow identity in slots in which they lost interest and enthusiasm years ago.

Repeat: *You are not your job title*—you are, in fact, a versatile, many-faceted being with a storehouse full of qualities that can relate to a large range of work positions. Whether student or secretary, engineer or executive, you most probably have a lot more going for you than you are willing to admit. Let's see if, together, we can dig some of this out.

THE BUILDING BLOCKS

As a human being you are endowed with, and have acquired, a large variety of personal and technical tools for dealing with the world around you. You have successfully developed thousands of routines or procedures for handling the day-to-day problems of life—*all* of life, from backyard to boardroom, from children to community, private life to professional life. These are your skills, abilities, and personal attributes. You wouldn't have made it this far if you didn't have them.

And, you have developed a pleasure profile. A shopping list of things that turn you on: puzzles that challenge you, sensations that tickle you, types of relationships that nurture you, environments in which you feel good, activities that contribute to your well-being and that of others.

All of the personal qualities, whether in the skill or interest family, can be seen as building blocks—elements out of which you can fashion your job target of the moment. But notice that if you knock down the structure, remove the job title, you haven't lost anything: the building blocks are still there intact—all of them, including many you weren't using in the last job, and perhaps forgot you had.

With knowledge of your personal building blocks you can construct another job title, or target. And by being able to identify and describe these personal components, you will create the central core of your perfect resume. (Personal data, work history, and education will be added later.)

THE FOUR BLOCKS

In the Career Discovery Process we analyze four primary building blocks that are very useful in your resume.

BLOCK ONE—YOUR SKILLS
BLOCK TWO—YOUR INTERESTS
**BLOCK THREE—YOUR PERSONAL
  ATTRIBUTES**
BLOCK FOUR—YOUR RESULTS

In the following pages you will explore each block or module, separately, with exercises, checklists, and procedures designed to put you in touch with ways of communicating about yourself in effective resume terms. By participating in these exercises you will actually be writing this book with us, and the result will be *your* perfect resume—not ours.

BLOCK ONE—YOUR SKILLS

There are two categories for you to look at here: *Basic Skills,* and *Specific Skills.* Basic Skills (writing, reading, driving, etc.) are the everyday foundations of our life in organized society and come primarily from early education. Many people tend to take these skills for granted, on the grounds that since "everyone can do this" why mention it? This is a mistake, as you will see.

Specific Skills (techniques) are the aspects of your abilities that most set you apart from others in your worklife. They are applications of your basic skills to the advancement of particular identifiable results. These techniques are not necessarily complicated or difficult; in fact they are normally fairly simple to describe. You may be surprised at the number you can come up with.

Basic Skills Checklist

Listed below is a cross-section of basic skills. Follow these instructions:

1. Read over the list, then check any box indicating that you feel you have a basic competence in this skill.

2. Add any other basic skills in which you are competent and that are not included.

3. After you have gone over the list once, go back, and for each skill you have checked, indicate whether you would be willing to use this skill in your work.

Check skills in which you are competent	Basic Skills	Check skills you are willing to use in your work
	Reading	
	Writing	
	Organizing	
	Communicating	
	Visualizing	
	Convincing Others	
	Working With Numbers	
	Imagining	
	Driving	
	Supporting Others	
	Cooking	
	Painting	
	Fast Learner	
	Traveling	
	Meeting Strangers	
	Dancing	
	Acting	
	Lifting Heavy Objects	
	Analyzing	
	Following Instructions	
	Living/Working Outdoors	
	Drawing	
	Counseling	
	Walking/Running	

Check skills in which you are competent	Basic Skills	Check skills you are willing to use in your work
	Managing Others	
	Remembering	
	Classifying	
	Innovating	
	Decorating	
	Working With Hands	
	Meeting Deadlines	
	Supervising	
	Research	
	Keeping Records	
	Working with Animals	
	Helping Others	
	Conceptualizing	
	Planning	
	Acknowledging Others	
	Building	
	Understanding New Things	
	Teaching	
	Singing	
	Physical Dexterity	
	Repairing	
	Entertaining	
	Using Tools	
	Growing Things	
	Caring for Children	

List here any other basic skills you possess that we haven't included in our list above.

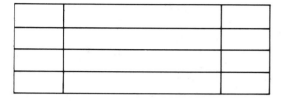
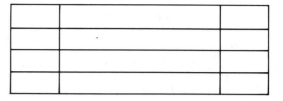

Your *Specific* Skills (Techniques)

These skills include job-related and non-job-related skills. Things you have learned to do in school, on your own, or at work. The general criterion is that when you apply the skill a specific measurable *result* is produced.

Typing letters would qualify as a specific skill because the *result* (the typed letter) is there. So would designing bridges, planning sales promotion campaigns, farming, fund raising, etc. A good way to inventory specific skills is to start with a basic skill and add specificity. Thus, the basic skill of *writing* could translate to specific skills in:

writing reports
writing letters
writing stories
writing employee evaluations
writing travel itineraries, etc.

The basic skill of *analyzing* can be made more specific as:

analyzing financial reports
analyzing office problems
analyzing work flow
analyzing personnel requirements
analyzing biological data

To start an inventory of your *specific skills,* go back over the list of basic skills you've checked off, and select the ten of these that you feel most qualified in and enjoy and are willing to use in your work. List each of the ten in one of the skill expansion boxes shown below and complete in accordance with the following four instructions:

Skill Expansion Boxes

1. List ten basic skills, each in one of the boxes provided after the examples given.

2. In each box, next list several other terms or expressions that are identical or similar to the basic skill listed, and write these terms under the basic skills.

3. Next list at least five specific ways that you *could* apply (or have applied) these skills in work or non-work activities. Don't limit yourself. Be expansive. You can edit later.

4. Keep listing specific skills until you have at least fifty statements, then list twenty-five of these statements (your choice) in Skill Summary Sheet One on page 30.

Sample

SKILL EXPANSION BOX

Basic Skill _Managing others_

Any other related terms which could describe this:

supervising   _directing others_

organizing people   _leading others_

Specific ways in which I could apply this skill:

supervising library projects

organizing our soft-ball team.

directing canvassing for political campaign

leading others to participate in fund-raising

managing church group to raise money over phone.

SKILL EXPANSION BOX #1

Basic Skill _____

Any other related terms which could describe this:

_____   _____

_____   _____

Specific ways in which I could apply this skill:

_____

_____

_____

_____

_____

SKILL EXPANSION BOX #2

Basic Skill _____

Any other related terms which could describe this:

_____   _____

_____   _____

Specific ways in which I could apply this skill:

_____

_____

_____

_____

_____

SKILL EXPANSION BOX #3

Basic Skill _____

Any other related terms which could describe this:

_____   _____

_____   _____

Specific ways in which I could apply this skill:

_____

_____

_____

_____

_____

SKILL EXPANSION BOX #4

Basic Skill _____

Any other related terms which could describe this:

_____   _____

_____   _____

Specific ways in which I could apply this skill:

_____

_____

_____

_____

_____

SKILL EXPANSION BOX #5

Basic Skill _____

Any other related terms which could describe this:

_____   _____

_____   _____

Specific ways in which I could apply this skill:

_____

_____

_____

_____

_____

_____

SKILL EXPANSION BOX #6

Basic Skill _____

Any other related terms which could describe this:

_____   _____

_____   _____

Specific ways in which I could apply this skill:

_____

_____

_____

_____

_____

SKILL EXPANSION BOX #7

Basic Skill _____

Any other related terms which could describe this:

_____   _____

_____   _____

Specific ways in which I could apply this skill:

_____

_____

_____

_____

_____

SKILL EXPANSION BOX #8

Basic Skill _____

Any other related terms which could describe this:

_____   _____

_____   _____

Specific ways in which I could apply this skill:

_____

_____

_____

_____

_____

SKILL EXPANSION BOX # 9

Basic Skill _____

Any other related terms which could describe this:

_____   _____

_____   _____

Specific ways in which I could apply this skill:

_____

_____

_____

_____

_____

SKILL EXPANSION BOX # 10

Basic Skill _____

Any other related terms which could describe this:

_____   _____

_____   _____

Specific ways in which I could apply this skill:

_____

_____

_____

_____

_____

Skill Summary Sheet One

Instructions:

1. Choose and list 25 specific skills
   from the Skill Expansion boxes
   (which are most valuable and
   enjoyable to you.
2. After you have listed all 25, check
   the appropriate boxes to the right.
3. (It is not necessary to list them in
   priority order).

	I would enjoy performing this skill	I consider myself to be qualified in this skill area	I have actual work or non-work experience in doing this	This is something I would be willing to explore further
1. _____				
2. _____				
3. _____				
4. _____				
5. _____				
6. _____				
7. _____				
8. _____				
9. _____				
10. _____				
11. _____				
12. _____				
13. _____				
14. _____				
15. _____				
16. _____				
17. _____				
18. _____				
19. _____				
20. _____				
21. _____				
22. _____				
23. _____				
24. _____				
25. _____				

So far, so good. You are building an inventory of the skills that you can offer to potential employers. The process doesn't add skills you didn't have, it simply clarifies. As you go through the process, you are becoming more articulate about the things you can do. Along the way you can deviate from our rules if you wish, and add extra criteria or additional skills whenever they occur. As you loosen up the resistance around the expression of your abilities, you should get a strong flow of valuable information about yourself—be sure to write it all down. You will use much of it in your resume.

Distillation

And now some sorting out. Review the twenty-five specific skills from Skill Summary Sheet One (page 30) and check ten that combine the most value for others and satisfaction for you. List them below in order of importance to you and your worklife.

Skill Summary Two

1. _____

2. _____

3. _____

4. _____

5. _____

6. _____

7. _____

8. _____

9. _____

10. _____

BLOCK TWO—YOUR INTERESTS

When we talk about your interests in this process, we aren't just talking about curiosity. What we are looking for goes beyond mere curiosity, and relaxed participation. We want more meat and blood in it. What are your turn-ons? What excites and challenges you? What would you walk a mile to do? Those interests.

And what would you like to know more about? What new games to learn how to play? How to create a greater sense of aliveness, health, happiness, love, full self-expression? In the work formula, we want you to see these personal pleasures in addition to skills. Actually they are already very parallel subjects: people tend to excel in the things they enjoy.

When you locate jobs that work for you, you start to understand what "making it" is all about. And it's not hard to do this in today's active, generating, techno-dynamic work flow. Not at all. Even in times of tight employment. The breakthrough, the transformation, comes when you are willing to actually be responsible for the quality of your worklife. Willing to have it your way. Interested? Continue following this process, and discover more.

Life and Work

Our mutual concern about interests in Block Two is not *directly* related to the resume you will produce. You don't feature interests on the resume—you feature the *value* you can provide to a prospective employer—the contribution you can make. However, you need to be conscious of your life interests so that the job targets you go after contain the underlying motive force that brings your life and your work together. Unfortunately, the stereotype from which most of us have obtained our beliefs about work is essentially this: *Work is what you do from nine to five, five days a week, and life starts after five and on weekends.* Work is what you *have* to do, and life is what you *want* to do. This is the attitude that floats around high school corridors and college dormitories like a virus, and permeates even the highest career ranks. The prevailing idea is that work is something to resist, a necessary evil, a struggle. Do as little as necessary, for as much as you can get.

Don't get sucked in by this. It ain't necessarily so! The only real struggle in work is put there by people who are not willing to be responsible for the quality of their life. Work and life happen at the same time. You are living 100 percent of the time when you are working, and can bring to work the same personal scope as you do to your playtime. It boils down to a question of choice: When you are in touch with your essential interests and motivations, and look out into the work world from this centered point of view, you begin to see work as *opportunity*—the opportunity to choose the games you want to play.

What does this have to do with your resume? Plenty. When you are in touch with your interests and turn-ons, as well as your skills and abilities, your resume becomes a passport to personal satisfaction rather than just a work permit.

Let's play.

The Pleasure Detector

Go down the activities listed below, and check off each one that could bring you a helping of personal pleasure. Don't stop to think when you read an item. If you get a small positive vibration, check it off even if you've never played the game before.

I like . . .

_____ to race cars, boats, horses	_____ to sing or act
_____ to go fishing	_____ taking care of sick people
_____ to work with machinery	_____ to arrange furniture
_____ to give parties	_____ to meet new people
_____ teen-agers	_____ to work with plants
_____ to be entertaining	_____ to play tennis
_____ dancing	_____ to make jewelry
_____ to give advice	_____ to drive a car
_____ sports	_____ to counsel families
_____ working alone	_____ to make cabinets
_____ going to the theater	_____ to collect art
_____ to take risks	_____ to read
_____ to do research in _____	_____ listening to music
_____ to be my own boss	_____ raising money for charity
_____ to attend meetings	_____ building things
_____ to persuade people	_____ problems in biology
_____ old people	_____ interviewing people
_____ routine, orderly tasks	_____ to buy things

_____ repairing furniture

_____ to teach

_____ to sell

_____ to analyze research reports

_____ taking care of animals

_____ to work at night

_____ taking care of children

_____ to decorate houses

_____ preparing a gourmet meal

_____ doing physical labor

_____ making a good bargain

_____ working with numbers

_____ negotiating a contract

_____ working for others

_____ designing clothes

_____ settling arguments

_____ organizational problem-solving

_____ to collect _____

_____ to do things outdoors

_____ navigating a sailboat

_____ sewing clothes

_____ supervising people

_____ solving people problems

_____ to collect stamps

_____ to help people

_____ religious activities

_____ to write reports

_____ to organize files

_____ merchandising

Fine—now write down any and all personal pleasures you can think of that aren't on our list.

_____   _____

_____   _____

_____   _____

How about your hobbies? Have they been covered? If not, write them in here.

_____   _____

_____   _____

If you had a guaranteed income of $100,000 per year for life without working, what would you do with your time? If not covered above, write these activities here.

_____   _____

_____   _____

Secret pleasures? Let the hedonist in you out. List anything else below even if you think it's slightly indulgent.

_____   _____

_____   _____

Pleasure Detector Synthesis

Now, synthesize. Go back over all of the items you came up with in The Pleasure Detector, and boil them down to those which you feel could bring the deepest personal satisfaction if you could blend them into your work.

Rank the ten personal interests you would most like to weave into your worklife or lifework.

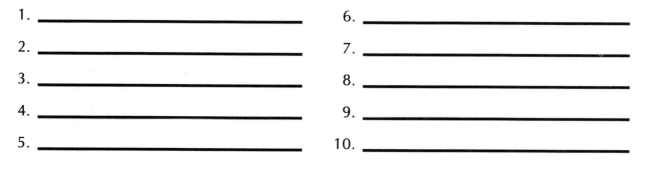

1. _____   6. _____

2. _____   7. _____

3. _____   8. _____

4. _____   9. _____

5. _____   10. _____

BLOCK THREE—YOUR PERSONAL ATTRIBUTES

Underneath your skills and interests there is still another you. That tenacious, irascible, courageous interface between the great world outside and the deep world inside, looking now one way and then the other in this adventure we call Life.

It is *you* they are hiring, not your made-up soap opera or the stereotype that you might have confused yourself with. And we know that it *looks* as if what they are interested in hiring is the stereotype or work role. As a matter of fact, that's probably what they think too. Actually, there is a stronger undercurrent at work. What it boils down to is a fairly concentrated essence of the good old American work ethic in its best form.

Employers want to hire. Applicants forget that and often fall back into an adversary, defensive posture. Organizations have one big underlying problem: to hire the right people to solve all of the other nit-picking problems and exploit the opportunities that define the purpose of the organization.

Employers know that in the really im-portant positions they need people not to hammer all the pegs into holes, or fill out endless reports, but *people who can get the job done,* who come from a position of *mastery,* and then learn to handle the details as they come along. Problem solvers. If one thing characterizes today's work world more than any other, it is the atmosphere or actionsphere of change. New techniques, new resource problems, worldwide political change, social change, lifestyle and workstyle changes.

There is no measure of this ability to master the job other than your own willingness and ability to say so. But carefully. Not to drop into bravado, or self-glorification, but to clearly demonstrate the qualities you have that will support the people you want to work for.

These are your *personal attributes.* Those ways of defining the part of you that is the context from which you operate. The generating principles that provide the power behind your work, sometimes called character. Do the personality profile on the following page to get more in touch with these attributes.

Personality Profile
INSTRUCTIONS

First, review the list of personal attributes below with yourself in mind. Not just the you that all of us know about, but also the one that you alone know about. Draw a line through all of the attributes that you feel are *not* really you, that you don't identify with. If you are on the fence about it, leave it in.

Then, go over the list again, and this time circle each term that describes an attribute clearly representing a facet of your persona.

Next, in the space provided, write in any basic personal characteristics that aren't on our list but that you feel describe you at least as well.

Willing	Perceptive
Able	Imaginative
Thorough	Creative
Precise	Fast
Careful	Diligent
Energetic	Intelligent
Honest	Intuitive
Hard-working	Determined
Dedicated	Forthright
Insightful	Tenacious
Assertive	Responsible
Sensitive	Persistent
Supportive	Incisive
Able to produce results	Warm
Trustworthy	Friendly
Intent	Humorous
Masterful	Intellectual
Communicative	Analytic
Helpful	Persuasive
Easygoing	Organized
Strong	Flexible

List any other attributes we didn't think of that apply to you:

_____   _____

_____   _____

_____   _____

Finally, select four of the personal attributes you circled—the most powerful four from your point of view—and list them in the space provided.

Primary Personal Attributes

FINAL SELECTION

I am:

1. _____

2. _____

3. _____

4. _____

Optional: Using the terms you have selected, write a two-paragraph description of yourself as it would appear in *Who's Who—Special Edition!*

BLOCK FOUR: YOUR RESULTS

Time to shift gears. We have been operating for the previous several pages in an exploratory, introspective manner, looking at ways of communicating tangibly some qualities that are not always clearly evident to the outside world. Now we want to turn the spotlight outward on your relationship with the physical universe—the world of results.

As used in this process, a result is a *tangible, measurable final product, achievement, or accomplishment that you have produced or created out of your involvement or participation in a particular activity or job.* Results go beyond hope or help, beyond reason and purpose, beyond theory or intention, beyond aspirations and goals, and beyond your job description. Results have a physical form. They are almost impossible to ignore. They are the precious stones in the setting of your resume. When you speak the language of results, people remember.

Compare these two statements:

• My duties included cost analysis, planning, work flow, scheduling construction activities, budgeting, and architectural design and engineering.

or:

• I designed the John Hancock Building in Boston.

Now close your eyes and see which one you can remember.

The more tangible results you have in your resume the easier it is to get a strong and memorable picture of your capacity to do the job you seek.

Results come in all shapes and sizes and relate to every area of activity in your life. People frequently take what they do so much for granted that, when asked to describe what results they have produced, they have difficulty coming up with any. They look for something significant or award-winning and, falling short of that, they fail to mention anything.

We are going to ask you to inventory some of the results you have produced in your life, to list anything you can think of, large or small. Allow yourself to free associate—write down anything that comes to mind, you can edit it later.

Results Inventory

In each category shown on the following pages write down as many past results and achievements you can think of. List whatever you think of even if you're not sure it fits that category, or even if you aren't sure that it's a result! Categories necessarily overlap. We have provided a few examples in each category to allow you to warm up to the pace.

SCHOOL RESULTS

Our examples

- Managed student blood drive—recruited twenty volunteers by myself
- Edited class yearbook
- Raised over $1,000 for local election
- Wrote fifteen-page report and analysis of *Future Shock,* by Alvin Toffler
- Earned over fifty dollars per week in part-time work while carrying a full daytime class load

List your results from school here:

_____

_____

_____

_____

_____

OTHER TRAINING RESULTS

Think of achievements in other areas of training or know-how.

Our examples

- Finished Katharine Gibbs steno course
- Completed AMA interviewing workshop
- Took Xerox sales-training program
- Graduated from est training

Yours

_____

_____

_____

TIME OFF RESULTS

List any results you have produced during vacation periods, times of unemployment, weekends, after hours, or other times off.

Our examples

- Managed state champion little league team
- Supervised ten-day camping trip for ten persons
- Designed costumes for three musicals at local summer tent theater
- Remodeled my apartment
- Learned ceramics in one summer
- Organized local political campaign

Yours

———————————————————————————————————

———————————————————————————————————

———————————————————————————————————

HOBBY RESULTS

List any results or accomplishments you have achieved with any hobbies you have.

Our examples

- Read complete works of Vladimir Nabokov
- Built a hundred-watt Heathkit amplifier
- Improved golf score from over one hundred to low nineties in one year
- Organized annual tennis tournament at work
- Made three very complicated quilts from patterns

Yours

———————————————————————————————————

———————————————————————————————————

———————————————————————————————————

MILITARY RESULTS

If you have had any military experience, look creatively at what the results were for you.

Our examples

- Mastered the F11F Guidance System
- Completed twelve USAFI training programs
- Served as supply clerk, organized system
- Supervised a detachment of twelve civilians
- Learned the German language

Yours

_____

_____

_____

COMMUNITY RESULTS

Where have you participated in community affairs and achieved something of value? Include volunteer and paid work.

Our examples

- Helped set up counseling program for aged
- Managed Hunger Project enrollment drive
- Organized opposition to town center building project
- Helped get mayor re-elected

Yours

_____

_____

_____

HOME RESULTS

Don't ignore the obvious achievements that you have been responsible for at home, particularly if you haven't had much paid work experience.

Our examples

- Helped remodel an old ten-room house
- Managed small family trust fund
- Repaired home appliances
- Prepared family tax returns
- Managed family budget

Yours

_____

_____

_____

WORK EXPERIENCE RESULTS

List up to three different jobs you have had (full-time, part-time, summer), starting with the most recent or most relevant and going back in importance. For each position list at least five achievements or results, even if they seem trivial now. Start with the ones you are proudest of.

If you have had little or no formal work experience, look for any project or position you have been involved with—in sports, recreation, travel, home management, working with people, politics, etc.

Our examples of the kinds of things to include as work results:

- Increased work flow by 20 percent
- Cut out three steps in paper cup production process
- Organized office personnel records
- Managed million-dollar acquisition
- Planned training agenda
- Set up career resource library

Yours (most recent work experience)

Position _____ Dates _____
Employer _____

List five accomplishments or results produced:

_____

_____

_____

_____

_____

Earlier work experience

Position _____ Dates _____
Employer _____

List five accomplishments or results produced:

_____

_____

_____

_____

_____

Earlier work experience

Position _____ Dates _____
Employer _____

List five accomplishments or results produced:

_____

_____

_____

_____

_____

MISCELLANEOUS RESULTS

List any achievements, final products, results, or solutions to problems that you haven't written down yet, and that you feel demonstrate your capabilities.

_____

_____

_____

THE TOP TEN

Go back and read over all of the work-related or non-work results you have listed from page 41 to page 46, selecting the ones you consider most relevant to your possible future work and grading them with check marks as follows:

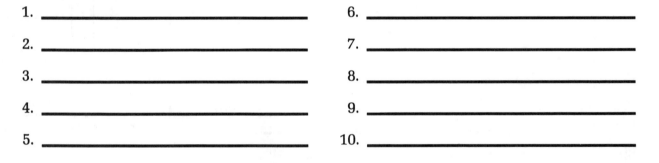

✓ not relevant to my future work
✓✓ somewhat relevant to my future work
✓✓✓ quite relevant to my future work

Be careful not to rate low any item in relevance simply because it may have occurred in a different field of work. If the way you accomplished the result could be relevant to your next work assignment, that will qualify it.

From the ones you have checked, select the ten past results that in your view are _most_ relevant to your future work.

1. _____   6. _____

2. _____   7. _____

3. _____   8. _____

4. _____   9. _____

5. _____   10. _____

Congratulations!

If you have completed the preceding analysis of the resume building blocks with integrity and consciousness, you have just gone further in preparation *for* your resume than at least 95 percent of your colleagues and competitors in the job market. You have made a major contribution to yourself and your work consciousness, and the results in your resume and job campaign will show it.

Possibly, you ran into some confusion or personal barriers along the way as you put the searchlight on yourself. This is not an easy process, and many people have difficulty in self-appraisal. Shortly we're going to show you how to summarize the information. Before you do that, however, if you feel you could improve what you've already done, go back over the lists again and add to them. Remember, it's *your* perfect resume we're after.

SUMMARIZING THE FOUR BLOCKS

You have now completed bringing to light and summarizing the four core components of your resume. (Your work history, education, and personal data will be discussed shortly, when you start the actual writing process.) Summarize below what you've captured so far.

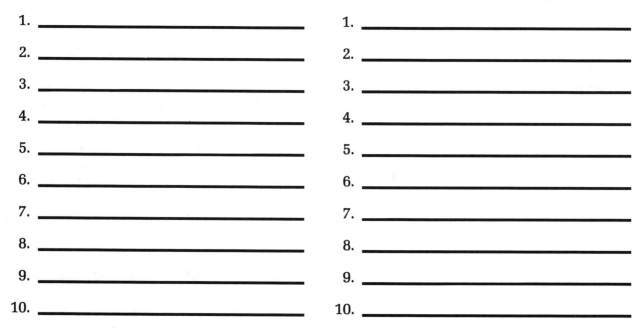

Block One: Your Skills

(You can pick these up from page 32.)

1. _____
2. _____
3. _____
4. _____
5. _____
6. _____
7. _____
8. _____
9. _____
10. _____

Block Two: Your Interests

(You can pick these up from page 36.)

1. _____
2. _____
3. _____
4. _____
5. _____
6. _____
7. _____
8. _____
9. _____
10. _____

Block Three: Your Personal Attributes

(You can pick these up from page 39.)

1. _____

2. _____

3. _____

4. _____

Block Four: Your Results

All of the above have combined to create the following major achievements and results in your life.
(You can pick these up from page 46.)

1. _____

2. _____

3. _____

4. _____

5. _____

6. _____

7. _____

8. _____

9. _____

10. _____

You now have the basic building blocks that will allow you to focus on job targets and a perfect resume to get you just what you want in the work world. This puts you in the top 10 percent of your career competitors . . . Be proud!

Job Targeting

If you are very clear about your personal job targets, you can skip this part, and move directly to page 63.

Imagine for a moment that you are an employer. Say, for example, that you are the manager of customer service for a small mini-computer firm. It is your job to ensure that any complaints or service requirements from purchasers of your equipment are satisfied promptly, professionally, and in a way that encourages customer loyalty.

As manager, you have six service representatives who are in communication with customers, primarily by phone, to a lesser degree by letter, and occasionally in person. One of your service reps is leaving, and you are screening candidates for his/her replacement. With your job requirement in mind, and knowing that you have a large pile of resumes to get through, read the following two resume paragraphs.

Yes—you guessed it—another before-and-after story. The same person with two different approaches to the same experience. In the second example the unnecessary details have been eliminated, and the switch made from chronological and "duty" oriented to a more targeted functional approach focusing on "results" in the sales and service aspects of a customer service job target.

Advantage: Greatly enhanced attention by the employer, and a probable interview.

By targeting his/her resume our candidate made it easy for the employer to notice the points of his/her experience that would be related to the employer's needs.

Like a good advertisement the resume works best when the writer has a clear idea of who the "prospect" is and what that person wants. It's that basic.

1976 - Present - Sales Trainee - Photo Ion, Inc.
                                 633 La Cienega Drive
                                 Los Angeles, California

As one of seven persons in the Sales department I was responsible

for dealing with customers on a variety of levels, in introducing

the Mark IV electronic photo copier in the Western five state

region (California, Nevada, Oregon, Washington, Colorado).

My duties included screening new prospects, setting up meetings,

assisting in sales calls, helping with installations and

responding to customer complaints.

Customer Service Experience

* Assisted in introduction of new electronic projects
   to customers in Western states.

* Worked with over fifty companies to increase acceptance
   and use of innovative copying system.

* Helped to reduce customer complaints by 50% in 90 days.

* Mastered complex equipment servicing in record time.

THE UNIVERSAL HIRING RULE

Any employer will hire any individual as long as the employer is convinced that the hiring will bring more value than its cost.

As we have said, contrary to popular opinion employers are very interested in hiring. That's their job: to locate the best people and equipment to get the work done. This is true in employment downturns as well as periods of high demand. Employers always need people who can produce results: *profits, safety, cost-cutting organization, solutions.* These words (and deeds) are music to the ears of any manager or supervisor who is under pressure to control the work flow in his/her department.

The disturbing difficulty from the vantage of guidance and career counselors is that most job candidates don't seem to understand the rules. Left to their own devices, the average job seekers more times than not will virtually obscure the major relevant points in their resumes with too much additional information, unclear writing style, and lack of direction.

Targeting your resume means to aim its thrust directly at the most obvious needs of a particular employment opportunity or job target. Without a clear idea of your job target you will be left in the position of having to cover too many bases, say too much that is not relevant, which, unfortunately, most don't have the time or inclination to do.

YOUR JOB TARGET

A job target is a particular work description or title in a given field. It is not a specific job opening, but rather a title that could exist with a number of employers. For example, *service rep, cost accountant, travel agent, legal secretary* are all job targets. Your resume will be dramatically more valuable and communica-

tive if it has been fashioned for a job target that you have worked out in advance. Once you are clear about the target, it becomes obvious what to include and what to leave out.

If you are organizing a thorough job campaign, you will probably have two or three job targets in related or, in some cases, different fields, reflecting sometimes diverse sets of interests and skills. In completing Part 1 of the Career Discovery Process you have unearthed much of what is needed to construct your job targets.

Our basic requirement for your job target is that it *starts with you.* You put it together out of your skills and interests. If you target job areas relating only to your skills, your work will miss that essential pleasure bond that keeps the juices of motivation and satisfaction flowing. On the other hand, if you go after areas of interest where there isn't a viable skill base, you won't have much to describe in your resume or interview.

A job target is something that you are aiming for. It lies along a course line, or lifeline, and can include a short-term job goal as well as a long-term career direction. For example, your three-year target could be as an employment manager, and your immediate job goal might be as an interviewer or recruiter.

With clear job targets you are in charge of your work search, and your resume reflects this clarity. Without a job target your approach to the employment market is mostly opportunistic and will involve many false starts, wrong turns, and dead ends. The extra work involved in targeting pays dividends in the ease of organizing your job search and resume, and of course the big payoff is that you end up in work that reflects who you are and brings you increased day to day satisfaction.

JOB TARGET LIST

If you are already very clear about one or more job targets for yourself, list them here:

My first job target is: _____

My second job target is: _____

My third job target is: _____

If these targets are completely satisfying
for you, move directly to page 63.

Job Target Creation

If you haven't pulled together your job targets yet, here is a short process that will help. Follow these instructions:

1. Go back to your list of specific skills on page 48 and select five major skills. List them below.

2. Also, list your five major interests from page 48.

Five Major Skills

_____

_____

_____

_____

_____

Five Major Interests

_____

_____

_____

_____

_____

3. Next, mix and match these skills and interests in some exploratory steps, which require you to step out of any preconceived ideas about your job title and uncover alternatives you might not have considered.

In the spaces below list pairs of skills and interests, and then come up with job titles that you feel combine these. Pick skills and interests that you feel could be tied together in a variety of job possibilities. Don't limit yourself only to combinations that reflect what you've already decided about yourself. And in coming up with the job titles, be willing to stretch your imagination a bit—list titles that may not be directly relevant to your idea of what you want to do. Play around!

Here are some examples of what we mean:

The skill of _negotiating_
and
The interest in _working with people_

could combine in the following job possibilities:
1. Labor negotiator
2. Arbitrator
3. Marriage counselor

The skill of _purchasing/buying_
and
The interest in _business systems_

could combine in the following job possibilities:
1. Office manager
2. Purchasing agent
3. Systems (planner)

The skill of _communication_
and
The interest in _travel_

could combine in the following job possibilities:
1. Travel agent
2. Tour guide
3. Convention planner

The skill of _typing and shorthand_
and
The interest in _dancing_

could combine in the following job possibilities:
1. Secretary to theatre manager
2. Assistant to dance instructor
3. Assistant editor—dance magazine

It's your turn: In the spaces below, write down skills and interests from your lists in combinations that could relate to work situations. You may use the same interests and skills more than once. (If you get stuck and need more, you may go back to your original skills and interests lists on pages 30 and 36. Don't stop until you have at least *twenty* job possibilities in the right-hand margin. Write things down even if your mind raises the red flags of "I can't" or "I won't."

could combine in the following job possibilities:

The skill of _____

    and

The interest in _____

1. _____
2. _____
3. _____

could combine in the following job possibilities:

The skill of _____

    and

The interest in _____

4. _____
5. _____
6. _____

could combine in the following job possibilities:

The skill of _____

    and

The interest in _____

7. _____
8. _____
9. _____

could combine in the following job possibilities:

The skill of _____

    and

The interest in _____

10. _____
11. _____
12. _____

could combine in the following job possibilities:

The skill of _____

    and

The interest in _____

13. _____
14. _____
15. _____

could combine in the following job possibilities:

The skill of _____

    and

The interest in _____

16. _____

17. _____

18. _____

could combine in the following job possibilities:

The skill of _____

    and

The interest in _____

19. _____

20. _____

21. _____

could combine in the following job possibilities:

The skill of _____

    and

The interest in _____

22. _____

23. _____

24. _____

could combine in the following job possibilities:

The skill of _____

    and

The interest in _____

25. _____

26. _____

27. _____

could combine in the following job possibilities:

The skill of _____

    and

The interest in _____

28. _____

29. _____

30. _____

And now list any other job possibilities that are worthy of consideration in your own career development:

_____

_____

_____

_____

_____

Selected Job Titles

If you had difficulty coming up with job titles to match your skills and interests, don't be alarmed, for many people have the same problem. The mind sometimes goes blank when confronted by the immensity of the work world.

To stimulate your thinking, here is a list of well over two hundred job titles selected from employment classified advertisements around the country. Read through them and let your mind expand upon these choices with your own ideas. If you get some new ideas from this list, you can add them to the job targets you came up with in the preceding pages. Then continue with the next part of the process.

Decorator	Telephone worker	Political aide
Greengrocer	Secretary	Geologist
Bus driver	College recruiter	Navigator
Lyricist	Billing clerk	Counselor
Speech therapist	Interior designer	TV producer
Private investigator	Locksmith	Oceanographer
Air traffic controller	Scuba instructor	Media planner
Exercise coach	Typesetter	Skier
Kite maker	Computer operator	Administrative assistant
Insurance agent	Guidance counselor	Die cutter
Biographer	Buyer	Inspector
X-Ray technician	Environmentalist	Journalist
Teller	Labor relations specialist	Lab technician
Occupational therapist	Hostess	College professor
Meteorologist	Underwriter	Career developer
Ambulance attendant	Trade journalist	Foreman
Home economist	Restaurant manager	Electrician
Inventory clerk	Diamond setter	Instructor
Jeweler	Illustrator	Landscape designer
Product manager	Linguist	Homemaker
Auditor	Security officer	Human resources specialist
Veterinarian	Programmer	Gal/guy Friday
Translator	Typist	Gamesperson
Bond analyst	Office manager	Executive
Entomologist	Lifeguard	Writer
Jockey	Bartender	Tennis pro
Sales representative	Banker	Geneticist
Orthopedist	Copywriter	Driver
Marketing coordinator	Dental hygienist	Exporter
Pilot	Lecturer	Chemist
Industrial relations manager	Zoologist	Florist
Actor/actress	Stenographer	Librarian
Keypunch operator	Recruiter	Biologist

Reservationist
Analyst
Attorney
Dentist
Interviewer
Legislator
Printer
Teacher
Medical technologist
Publisher
Accountant
Credit manager
Optician
Payroll clerk
Stockbroker
Toy designer
Program analyst
Receptionist
Horse dealer
Legal aid specialist
Fund raiser
Bookkeeper
Anthropologist
Demographer
Customer service
Social director
Research assistant
Hotel manager
Ecologist
Data processor
Broker
Comptroller
Actuary
Dietician
Travel agent
Novelist
Social worker
Pharmacist
Newscaster
Musician
Account executive
Critic

Dancer
Farmer
Correspondent
Machinist
Product manager
Mechanic
Tool and die maker
Paralegal
Sound engineer
Physical therapist
Superintendent
Reporter
Politician
Messenger
Agriculturist
Designer
Economist
Budget manager
Consumer advocate
Tax specialist
Projectionist
Retailer
Salesperson
Nurse
Masseuse/masseur
Animal scientist
Cryptographer
Fashion model
Architect
Estimator
Botanist
Switchboard operator
Photographer
Producer
Mailroom clerk
Career counselor
Market researcher
Caseworker
Nutritionist
Management consultant
Proofreader
Set designer

Carpenter
Financial analyst
Physician
Supervisor
Engineer
Artist
Management trainee
Audio-visual aide
Mortician
Negotiator
Audiologist
Cashier
Editor
Caterer
Flight attendant
Cartographer
Food scientist
Photo journalist
Clerk typist
Media analyst
Claims adjustor
Maintenance person
Psychologist
Systems analyst
Chef
Furniture maker
Executive secretary
Composer
Collector
Family planner
Packaging expert
Child care worker
Geographer
Manager
Physicist
Statistician
Public relationist
Columnist
Inventor
Commentator
Marketeer
Communications specialist

4. Narrow down.

The idea now is to take your expanded exploratory job possibility lists. Select ten to twelve possibilities and narrow them down to a more personal reality. Go back over the list and transcribe each to the appropriate column below related to your present idea of the amount of satisfaction this title could provide you if you were working in it.

Very Satisfying	Somewhat Satisfying	Not Satisfying
————————	————————	————————
————————	————————	————————
————————	————————	————————
————————	————————	————————
————————	————————	————————
————————	————————	————————
————————	————————	————————
————————	————————	————————
————————	————————	————————

Then rank the titles in each column in accordance with how "practical" you feel this title would be as a real job target for you. You can use any meaning you wish to define this practicality for yourself. Enter a separate set of numbers in each column.

5. Bottom Line.

If all went well, and you pushed through the complexities of this targeting process, you have handled several very important variables that underlie your perfect resume: *skill, interest, satisfaction,* and *practicality.*

You should know that by following this job targeting process you have already exercised more work consciousness than most of the population. You have gotten closer to job targets that represent the essential you and that can produce the satisfaction and aliveness that turn work into play.

Finally, reduce your list to two or three job targets that you would be willing to go after with energy, and in the pursuit of which you would be *willing* to prepare a perfect resume. You may make this final selection by using any criteria you wish. We've taken you this far—you make the final choice on your own terms and list the selections on the following page.

MY JOB TARGETS ARE:

First job target _____

Second job target _____

Third job target _____

Now read what you've written above and see if you feel satisfied with the decision you have made. If not, track backward through the process and modify any choices you made. When you are confident about your selections, acknowledge yourself and move along to the next part of the resume process.

YOU BE THE JUDGE— BEFORE

Shown below is an actual resume from a person who wrote it without any clarity about his job target. Pretend to be an employer and read it with a view toward understanding how the person could assist you.

Turn the page for a revised version of the same person's resume.

RESUME

Frederick L. Mannes　　　27 Beyer Court, Rhinebeck, N.Y.　　　914-242-8874

Experience

Boston Gear International - LABOR RELATIONS MANAGER - June 1974-Present.

Did main work in personnel department with duties which included the following functions: Labor relations, negotiations, wage and salary decisions, interviewing and safety considerations. Was also responsible for management of personnel office, supervising the department. This position was a promotion from previous position in Purchasing Department for more responsibility.

General Merchandising Corp.- PERSONNEL ADMINISTRATOR - Feb. 1972 - May 1974

Was responsible for all the phases of administration in the personnel dept. Also took courses in sales and marketing while employed here, and increased my knowledge of company methods. Heavy phone contact and correspondence.

United Pump Mfg.- ASSISTANT PERSONNEL MANAGER - June 1969-Jan. 1972

Held responsible position of personnel manager's assistant and performed all of her many functions when she was absent, ill or away. Dealt with employees and potential employees. This was a high pressure position.

Do-Well Employment Agency, Inc.- COUNSELOR - March 1968-April 1969

This was a company which placed over 200 people in permanent positions each year and also handled temporary placements. We specialized in clerical and Secretaries. Learned about hiring practices in the metro area.

Education

B.S. from Fordham University, Majored in Biology with Minor in Theatre, 1967
Graduated - Central City High School - National Honor Society 1963
Rider Academy - Received Special Scholastic Award in Science Finished 1959

Personal

Married: 2 dependent children
Health: Excellent

References available on request.

YOU BE THE JUDGE—   AFTER

Here is the resume that the same person wrote after becoming clear about his primary job target and using some of the procedures in this book. (Incidentally, he also prepared a different resume for his secondary job target as college recruiter.)

Frederick L. Mannes
27 Beyer Court
Rhinebeck, N.Y. 11293
914-242-8874

Job Target: Employee Benefit Executive

Abilities: .Direct a comprehensive employee benefits programs for over
30,000 employees
.Negotiate contracts with insurance and other benefits personnel
.Manage labor relations negotiations and pre-negotiating planning
.Analyze health-care programs for cost-effectiveness
.Research both salaried and hourly benefits programs
.Closely monitor federal, state and local legislation and identify
potential labor problems
.Accurately and clearly communicate details of benefits programs
to both employer and employees

Achievements: .Developed employee benefits programs for over 250 hourly employees
.Negotiated benefits contracts resulting in 17% savings on premiums
.Identified potential problems in new legislation, thus avoiding
several potentially costly lawsuits
.Directed research on major new medical benefits program
.Set cost-control standards which have since been adopted
throughout pump industry
.Developed new kit for use in communicating benefits program
to hourly employees

Work History:

1974-Present   Boston Gear International - Labor Relations Manager

1972-1974   General Merchandising Corporation - Personnel Administrator

1969-1972   United Pump Manufacturing - Assistant Personnel Manager

1968-1969   Employment Counselor

Education:

B.A. Fordham University 1967

PREPARING THE PERFECT RESUME

Step 1: Selecting Your Resume Format

Now that you have discovered, or redis-covered, or affirmed (or just settled for) your job targets and have completed—or bypassed—the Career Discovery Process, you are ready to put your resume together and start to handle the nitty gritty (impor-.tant technical details) of its preparation. The steps are simple and the instructions clear, so go to it and have fun. The work you are doing will pay off handsomely in the final product.

In the best modern architectural and de-sign studios you will frequently hear the expression *form follows function* bandied about. Manufacturing and organizational experts use it too. The contemporary ap-proach is to create structures that effi-ciently accomplish their purpose, without unnecessary ornamentation or outdated stereotypes.

The same principle applies with equal validity to your resume. For best results you should start with a form or format that reflects the particular demands or re-quirements of your own job targets and work history.

If you haven't had much experience with resumes, it might surprise you to learn that there are actually as many as five possible formats for your resume. If you've had a lot of experience with re-viewing resumes, the surprise might be that there are *only* five, since from an em-ployer's point of view it seems that the varieties are endless—sometimes hope-less!

In fact, although there are many differ-ent *layouts,* there are really only five basic resume formats that you need to know. These are:

CHRONOLOGICAL FORMAT

Work experience and personal history ar-ranged in reverse time sequence.

FUNCTIONAL FORMAT

Work experience and abilities catalogued by major areas of involvement—some-times with dates, sometimes without.

TARGETED FORMAT

A highly focused presentation of your abilities and accomplishments directed to a very specific job target.

RESUME ALTERNATIVE

A special purpose communication for peo-ple for whom a resume isn't appropriate due to lack of experience.

CREATIVE ALTERNATIVE

A free form approach for artsy-craftsy folk.

RESUME FORMATS DESCRIBED

CHRONOLOGICAL

Notice that in this resume the job history is spelled out from the most recent job backward—with the most recent job having the most space. Titles and organizations are emphasized and duties and accomplishments within those titles described.

Advantages: emphasizes continuity and career growth. Highlights name of employer. Easy to follow.

Best used: when your career direction is clear and the job target is directly in line with your work history or name of last employer adds strong prestige.

JACK DEUTSCH
415 Sommer Road
Warwick, New York 94226
(914) 968-6357

WORK EXPERIENCE:

1975-Present   GOODSON APPAREL INDUSTRIES, INC.
                New York, New York

                Divisional Controller: Reported directly to the
                Chief Financial Officer. Managed cash funds; pre-
                pared consolidated corporate tax returns for seven
                companies and financial review of major subsidiaries.
                Designed and prepared a monthly sales comparison
                report for corporate executives. Co-supervisor of
                a 12 member staff that handled all facets of accounting
                for a 25 million dollar company.

1974-1975   STACEY'S, INC.
                New York, New York

                Corporate Auditor: Reported directly to the Assistant
                Corporate Controller. Conducted operational and
                financial audits within the Treasurer's Office and
                five operating divisions. Developed a report with
                findings and recommendations for the CEO of each
                division and numerous management personnel.

1967-1974   PRICE, WETHERAU & COMPANY
                Certified Public Accountants
                New York, New York

                Supervising Senior: Joined the professional staff
                as an assistant accountant. Reported directly to
                partners and managers. Planned, supervised and com-
                pleted numerous audit assignments.

AWARDS; ACCREDITATIONS; MEMBERSHIPS:

1971   Certified Public Accountant, New York State
1967   Peter K. Ewald Award in Taxation
        American Institute of Certified Public Accountants
        New York State Society of Certified Public Accountants

EDUCATION:

1967   B.S. in Accounting   Hofstra University

FUNCTIONAL

This format highlights major areas of accomplishment and strength and allows you to organize them in an order that most supports your work objectives and job targets. Actual titles and work history are in a subordinate position and sometimes left off entirely.

Advantages: gives you considerable flexibility in emphasis. Eliminates repetition of job assignments. Tends to de-emphasize experience.

Best used: in cases of career change or redirection or first job search, or re-entry into the job market. When experience is hinted or when you wish to play up a particularly strong area of ability.

MARILYN M. GUNTER
792 Cliff Ct.
Portland, Oregon 97208
(503) 249-8862

INSURANCE LAW

    Advised management of insurance company on legality of insurance
    transactions. Studied court decisions and recommended changes
    in wording of insurance policies to conform with law and/or to
    protect company from unwarranted claims. Advised claims department
    personnel of legality of claims filed on company to insure against
    undue payments. Advised personnel engaged in drawing up of legal
    documents, such as insurance contracts and release papers.

CORPORATE LAW

    Extensive study of corporation structure, including legal rights,
    obligations and privileges. Acted as agent for several corporations
    in various transactions. Studied decisions, statutes and ordinances
    of quasi-judicial bodies.

REAL ESTATE LAW

    Handled sale and transfer of real property. Instituted title searches
    to establish ownership. Drew up deeds, mortgages, and leases. Acted
    as trustee of property and held funds for investment.

WORK EXPERIENCE

    1971-Present   COMMERCIAL AUTOMOBILE UNDERWRITER'S COMPANY, INC. -
                    Insurance Services Office Supervisor

EDUCATION

    1979   LLB University of Oregon Law School - Insurance Law,
            Corporate Law, Estate Planning, Income Taxation

    1971   B.A. University of Oregon

TARGETED

This format is best for focusing on a clear, specific job target (you would have a different one for each target). It lists only capabilities and supporting accomplishments that relate to the job target listed at the top.

Advantages: it makes a very impressive case for the one selected job, at the expense of other areas. It demonstrates a strong understanding and ability in the targeted area.

Best used: only when you are clear about your job targets and willing to go for them.

DAVID S. GILLIAM
712 Olive Street
Smithtown, New York 11829
914-228-0263

Job Target: Architect for Private Firm

ABILITIES:

- providing professional services in research, development and design of large complex of buildings
- providing design for alterations and renovations of many styles of architecture
- full design start to finish of large fast food facilities, adaptable to many locales
- designing libraries with special consideration to sound and lighting desig
- designing shopping centers, particularly in semi-tropical climates
- designing drive-in and walk-up banks
- designing hospital and rest home facilities conforming to full health and safety standards

ACHIEVEMENTS:

- design and construction of all county buildings and alterations thereto
- planned, organized, directed and reviewed all architectural and engineering functions of my department's jurisdiction
- designed office buildings, data processing facilities, health centers, courts, police stations, power plants, access roads and other facilities
- produced schematics, feasibility studies, reports and cost estimates
- designed schools, libraries and rest homes

WORK HISTORY:

1969-Present - Nassau County Department of Buildings and Grounds - County Architect
1962-1969 - Carl N. Tyne & Associates - Associate Architect

PROFESSIONAL AFFILIATIONS:

Corporate member - A.I.A.
Member - New York State Association of Architects

EDUCATION:

1960 - Nassau County Community College
License State of New York 1961

RESUME ALTERNATIVE

This is a detailed letter to a particular employer, addressing areas where you can be of value to that employer. It *demonstrates* your abilities as much as it describes them. It provides enough factual information to avoid the need for a resume, hopefully.

Advantages: creates employer interest without requiring a full resume. Addresses particular researched needs.

Best used: by people who have little or no work experience or background, who are willing to do the required research for each letter.

27 East Hartley Avenue
Bristol, New Hampshire 03222
January 20, 1980

Mr. Alfred Tolliver
TELEMANAGEMENT
2050 M St. N.W.
Washington, D.C. 20026

Dear Mr. Tolliver:

I believe my extensive experience in microwave together with analog and digital equipment would aid your consulting tasks. Some of my recent accomplishments are:

Managed a European Nodal Re-engineering and Test program consisting of 34 tropo/los sites. Performed site surveys, developed and prepared new profiles and reports (including NBS calculations) to satisfy government contract requirements. Contract was completed within budget requirements and maintainability and reliability was improved 15%.

Managed the transmission group and supervised three subsystems engineers' efforts required to implement a new specialized common carrier microwave system. System is performing satisfactorily and will be expanded in the near future.

Supervised all aspects of several field installations including acceptance tests of new terrestrial and dedicated specialized government systems. Systems were completed within cost allocations and have operated satisfactorily for many years.

My education includes a degree from Stevens Institute of Technology and telecommunication courses on company and manufacturers' premises.

I would like to meet with you and see how I might make a contribution to your organization. I will call you in a week or so.

Very truly yours,

Sanford A. Scribne
(603) 346-5297

CREATIVE ALTERNATIVE

Not for everyone, the creative resume tosses customary forms to the winds and demonstrates a highly polished individual approach. It should be used only in areas where this kind of creativity is related to the job target. Unless extremely well done, this approach can flop miserably. When done with great skill, it works very well.

Advantages: it gets read and frequently circulated to others. Makes one or two main points very clearly. Form can be varied indefinitely.

Best used: by writers, artists, theatrical design, public relations, and media persons.

SELECTION PROCESS

Listed below are summaries of advantages and disadvantages of each type of resume we have covered. Check each statement that applies to you, then select the format best for you. If you are still unclear about which format to choose, try doing a couple of approaches and comparing the results when you get to Step 2. For further clarity we have included another set of examples on pages 154 to 194.

CHRONOLOGICAL

IS Advantageous

_____ When name of last employer is an important consideration

_____ When staying in same field as prior jobs

_____ When job history shows real growth and development

_____ When prior titles are impressive

_____ In highly traditional fields (education, government)

Is NOT Advantageous

_____ When work history is spotty

_____ When changing career goals

_____ When you have changed employers too frequently

_____ When you wish to de-emphasize age

_____ When you have been doing the same thing too long

_____ When you have been absent from the job market for a while

_____ When you are looking for your first job

FUNCTIONAL

IS Advantageous	Is NOT Advantageous

IS Advantageous

_____ When you want to emphasize capabilities not used in recent work experience

_____ When changing careers

_____ When entering job market for first time

_____ Re-entering job market after an absence

_____ If career growth in past has not been good

_____ When you have had a variety of different, relatively unconnected work experiences

_____ Where much of your work has been free-lance, consulting, or temporary

Is NOT Advantageous

_____ When you want to emphasize a management growth pattern

_____ For highly traditional fields such as teaching, ministerial, political, where the specific employers are of paramount interest

_____ Where you have performed a limited number of functions in your work

_____ Your most recent employers have been *highly* prestigious

TARGETED

Includes most of the advantages and disadvantages of the functional resume and these further considerations:

IS Advantageous

_____ When you are very clear about your job target

_____ You have several directions to go and want a different resume for each

_____ You want to emphasize capabilities you possess, but may not have paid experience in

Is NOT Advantageous

_____ When you want to use one resume for several applications

_____ You are not clear about your capabilities and accomplishments

_____ When you are just starting your career and have little experience

RESUME ALTERNATIVE

IS Advantageous

_____ When you have had little or no work experience

_____ When you have been out of the job market for a long time

_____ When you are willing to do solid research on a particular *employer* of interest

_____ When you know or can find out the name of the person who will make the hiring decision

Is NOT Advantageous

_____ When you have had enough experience to warrant a functional or chronological resume

_____ If you have not decided what you want to do

_____ If you are not clear about the contribution you can make to an organization

CREATIVE ALTERNATIVE

IS Advantageous

_____ In fields in which written or visual creativity are prime requisites of the job

_____ The medium or your work is appropriate to a printed form

Is NOT Advantageous

_____ If you are planning to go through personnel

_____ If you are not very sure of your creative ability

_____ If you are looking for a management position

It's your move. After having reviewed the five resume formats and checked all of the appropriate boxes for advantages and disadvantages, which format do you wish to follow? (Note: It's possible to do more than one.) Check the appropriate line below for the resume format you feel will best represent you.

_____ Chronological Resume

_____ Functional Resume

_____ Targeted Resume

_____ Resume Alternative

_____ Creative Alternative

Step 2: Power Paragraphs

Now the pace quickens, as you move from the introspective and elusive definitions of your essential qualities and work purposes into the more tangible task of actually writing your resume. Your investment in yourself will pay off in more clarity and direction in your resume and in your over-all job search.

At this point you have chosen two or three job targets and a format that would best communicate your accomplishments and skills. Here in Step 2 you will learn the basic writing rules that apply to your resume. And in Step 3 you will write the first draft of your own perfect resume.

An Advertisement for Yourself

Your resume is not a biography or memoir. It is not a detailed history of your life and times. Perhaps, surprisingly, it is not even an application for employment. A perfect resume is a well-structured, easy-to-read presentation of your capabilities and accomplishments, designed to convince a potential employer to invite you for an interview. A self-advertisement.

Designed to convince? Is it aggressive, bragging, immodest? No, not at all—despite the recurring culturally reinforced fears that seem to condemn self-acknowledgment and ability. We are continually surprised to run into students, workers, and even career counselors who take the position that job seekers should *underplay* their enthusiasm, avoid direct statements of personal ability. To substitute the reluctant "I would like to try" for the imperative "I can!" Bad advice. If you have doubts, the question to ask is: How does the organization I am applying to describe *its* services or products? Do they hide their strengths? Play down their capabilities? Obscure their primary accomplishments? If so, we're willing to have you take the soft line. But frankly, we don't know many of these. On the contrary, we find that the most productive and exciting organizations have very little hesitancy to let you know who they are and what they can do.

And we're not talking about *hype* or inflated self-praise or lies. We are talking about a clear, unembarrassed portrayal of yourself, presented in the best possible light. The picture of you with all systems go, and all the stops off. You know who we mean—that side of you that wakes up to the challenge, that surprises your friends and family. That's the person we want you to write about. Leave out the parts about the warts and pimples, the times when you turned the wrong corner and forgot to set the alarm.

The One-Page Rule

A famous speaker and trainer once said that if you are willing to stay with the major points, you can tell your whole life story in two minutes, and still have time left over for questions. You may not yet be at that level of communication, but without question, regardless of your experience or education, you can present everything you need to say in your resume within one page.

Yes, one page—even though you have had six jobs and three degrees. In over a dozen years of reading and correcting resumes in the uncounted thousands, we have not yet found one that didn't work better on one page. As most great writers, architects, and advertising agencies know, *less is more.*

When you eliminate the repetitions, reinforcements, and redundancies, what is left communicates. Anyone who has had to read stacks of mail will recognize the satisfaction and clarity of a short letter that makes its point, compared with the resistance to a two- or three-page document. The shorter presentation emphasizes the important information.

Although it hasn't been scientifically documented, most personnel people agree that a two-page resume reduces readability and retention by 25 to 30 percent. As for a three-page resume, forget it. Readership is down by nearly half. An axiom of most resume experts is that very frequently the poorer, less confident candidates have the longest resumes.

Exception to the One-Page Rule

If you have written a variety of articles or books, received an impressive list of honors or awards, obtained a dozen or so patents, or worked on a number of recognizable products, and the knowledge of the details of this long list would be valuable in convincing an employer to see you, then you might want to consider an *addendum* to your resume in the form of a separate listing of these specific activities. The important thing is to make it clear that your resume *ends* on the first page, and that the attachment is more of a laundry list of examples rather than part of the page-one story.

At the bottom of the first sheet try a statement like: "list of publications attached" so that it's clear that if the recruiter wishes he can get the full story without turning to the addendum.

Methods for paring the excess fat from your resume and strengthening your one-page presentation.

1. Shorten sentences. Eliminate long windups and connections. For example, the sentence "I was the person chosen to coordinate the college fund-raising team for the homecoming week" can be restated as "Coordinated college fund-raising team."

2. Eliminate repetitions. If you did similar tasks in two or three different jobs, explain in detail only in most recent position.

3. Don't spell out information that is already implied or included in other information. If you are a college graduate, there is little reason to describe your high school education.

4. Leave off company addresses or names of references (you can provide at the interview if requested). You don't even have to state "references provided on request." This is assumed.

5. List only most recent positions. If you have a large number of past jobs, summarize the earliest with a statement like "1960–70, A variety of drafting positions."

6. Eliminate extraneous information. Employers don't need to know your weight, height, sex, marital status, health, children's names, church affiliations or social clubs or fraternities. If and when they need the information (that which is legal), they will get it in the interview or application, or later.

7. Condense. Don't give three examples when one will suffice.

Action and Accomplishments

Most resumes make dull reading—a sure cure for even the severest cases of insomnia. The problem: a limp narrative style that focuses on routine duties and responsibilities and ends up sounding like descriptions from a civil service job announcement. Puts people to sleep. What keeps employers awake are words and phrases that create pictures they can see in their mind's eye. Word pictures.

To create vivid word pictures that will keep potential employers awake, you need to combine two prime ingredients: *active verbs* to start sentences and paragraphs, and descriptions of the *results* you have produced in the work you have done, rather than just the duties you have performed. For example:

Limp style: My duties included the preparation and organization of sales information for use by management. In my performance of these duties I was able to make major improvements in the procedures that were used . . . etc.

Action style: Reorganized and operated new sales reporting system that provided increased information in half the time.

An accomplishment is nothing more than a *result,* a final measurable product that people can relate to. A duty is not a result, it is an obligation—every jobholder has duties. What really scores are the *results,* the accomplishments. Use as many as you can in your resume, or in any communication you make about yourself in your job campaign.

You have produced results in other aspects of your life—school, church, homelife, hobbies. Use everything you can find to demonstrate that you are in fact a *producer*, not just another dutiful worker.

And start sentences with action verbs to stimulate the reader's appetite to learn more about you.

EXERCISE YOUR POWER WRITING SKILLS

Below is a sample list of action verbs. Go down the lists and check those you feel could be used in sentences or paragraphs to describe *your* accomplishments.

ACTION VERBS

Created	Purchased	Rendered	Obtained	Increased
Instructed	Oversaw	Instructed	Studied	Expanded
Reduced (losses)	Installed	Counseled	Improved	Trained
Negotiated	Routed	Received	Consolidated	Devised
Planned	Corresponded	Built	Ordered	Supplied
Sold	Audited	Detected	Invented	Prepared
Completed	Coordinated	Selected	Diagnosed	Maintained
Designed	Researched	Logged	Examined	Interpreted
Consulted	Implemented	Recommended	Lectured	Administered
Evaluated	Presented	Distributed	Processed	Interviewed
Calculated	Instituted	Arranged	Reviewed	Advised
Identified	Directed	Disproved	Translated	Discovered
Performed	Managed	Developed	Prescribed	Restored
Constructed	Eliminated	Edited	Charted	Conserved
Controlled	Provided	Wrote	Represented	Delivered
Dispensed	Solved	Analyzed	Promoted	Arbitrated
Formulated	Determined	Produced	Recorded	Criticized
Improved	Collected	Conducted	Operated	Assembled
Tested	Referred	Delivered	Supervised	Realized
Protected	Served	Founded	Drew up	Navigated
Obtained	Compounded	Assisted	Organized	Reviewed

If there are any action words which clearly apply to you, and are not on our list, add them.

_____   _____   _____   _____   _____   _____

KEY PARAGRAPHS

Now take the action words and job phrases you have selected and, starting with each, write a short paragraph or long sentence describing a personal or work-related accomplishment or result you have produced. Do a minimum of three.

Action word or phrase

_____

_____

_____

_____

Action word or phrase

_____

_____

_____

_____

Action word or phrase

_____

_____

_____

_____

Go back over these accomplishment paragraphs now, and see if they can be edited to make them clearer or more powerful. Can you cut out some words and say the same things?

Some More Resume-Writing Rules

- Keep sentences and paragraphs *short* (no paragraph of more than ten lines).
- Use indented and "bulleted" statements (with • or * before each) where appropriate rather than complete sentences.
- Use simple terms rather than complex expressions that say the same thing.
- Use quantities, amounts, dollar values where they enhance the description of what you did ("increased sales by $100,000 per year").
- Put strongest statements at the top, working downhill from that.
- Have someone with good English skills check for spelling, punctuation, and grammar.
- Avoid excessive use of "I."
- Do not include hobbies or avocational or social interests unless they clearly contribute to your work abilities.
- Avoid purely personal evaluations.
  "I am an intelligent and diligent researcher"—is to be avoided. *"I have finished three major research projects"*—would be included.
- Don't go overboard with esoteric jargon. Remember that unenlightened people may have to understand you too.

Some Resume Don'ts

- Don't include pictures.
- Don't list references or relatives.
- Don't put resume in fancy binders or folders.
- Don't forget phone number, area code, zip.
- Don't list sex, weight, health, or other personal irrelevancies.
- Don't highlight problems (divorce, hospitalization, handicaps).
- Don't include addresses of prior employers (city and state are okay).
- Don't include salary information in your resume.

Final Reminders

Remember that the reason employers get interested in you is the value you can produce for them. This value is demonstrated by what you have done as much as by what you can do. Eliminate things that don't focus on your potential value. Above all, remember that your resume is a demonstration of your ability to handle written communication. Put as much care and attention into it as you would for a one-page advertisement for a fine product.

Step 3: The Facts

As we have already stated several times, the purpose of your resume is to serve as a concise advertisement of your ability to create value and results: Your "history" is actually not the *primary* concern, it's your ability to get the job done.

Facts are not capabilities, as many a disappointed employer has learned. The fact that you have put in five years with another firm doing a particular task doesn't ensure your performance on the next job. With an increasing reluctance of employers to give other than perfunctory references of past employees, the *fact* of employment may only mean that's where you hung your hat and collected your paycheck. However, the *facts* must be there, and reflected accurately and appropriately in a way that supports your capabilities.

On the following pages we are going to ask you to complete a rather substantial fact inventory that covers the following key areas about yourself:

Education and training
Military experience
Community work
Homework
Hobbies
Part-time jobs
Full-time jobs
Honors and awards
References

When you have completed this self inventory, you will have probably collected more information than you *or* most employers are interested in knowing. That's how it should be. We believe in accumulating a large data base of information, and then reducing and distilling what you've got into the key points. Be willing to take the extra time to complete it all. It will come in handy now and in the future—for resumes *and* employment applications.

YOUR RESUME INVENTORY

Fill out the following inventory of factual information. Not all of it may be required in your resume, but the information could be helpful to take with you to an interview or to fill out an application.

Education and Training

High School

If you are a college graduate you will probably not use this information on your resume, but you could need it for application forms.

School _____

Dates attended _____ to _____ Graduated _____

Major studies _____ Class standing _____

Honors and awards _____

Best subjects _____

Jobs held while in high school and during summers _____

_____

Other achievements and activities _____

_____

_____

College (undergraduate)

School _____

Dates attended _____ to _____ Graduated _____

Major studies _____ Class standing _____

Honors and awards _____

Best subjects _____

Extracurricular activities _____

_____

Jobs held while in college and during summers _____

_____

_____

Other achievements and activities _____

_____

_____

College (postgraduate, law school, medical school, etc.)

School _____

Dates attended _____ to _____ Graduated _____

School _____

Dates attended _____ to _____ Graduated _____

Major studies _____ Class standing _____

Honors and awards _____

Best subjects _____

Extracurricular activities _____

_____

Jobs held while in graduate school and during summers _____

_____

_____

Other achievements and activities _____

_____

_____

Other Training

(List any vocational courses, on-job training, military, or other formal training.)

Course _____ Date taken _____

Skills learned _____

_____

Course _____ Date taken _____

Skills learned _____

Course _____ Date taken _____

Skills learned _____

_____

Licenses or certificates held _____

_____

Home and Community Work

Activities you have done at home for self and family which demonstrate your abilities. *Don't undervalue this experience.*

Accomplishment _____

Skills demonstrated _____

_____

Accomplishment _____

Skills demonstrated _____

Accomplishment _____

Skills demonstrated _____

Hobbies

These reveal skills as well.

Hobby or activity _____

Accomplishment _____

Skills demonstrated _____

_____

Hobby or activity _____

Accomplishment _____

Skills demonstrated _____

Part-Time Jobs

Job _____ From/to _____

Employer _____

Accomplishments _____

Skills demonstrated _____

_____

Job _____ From/to _____

Employer _____

Accomplishments _____

Skills demonstrated _____

_____

Full-Time Employment

List each major position held even if several are with same employer. Be sure to include *at least one* accomplishment for each position. (Note: You should start with your earliest and work up to most recent even though this order will be reversed if you do a chronological resume.)

19 _____ to _____ Position and title _____

Employer _____ Location _____

Accomplishments _____

_____

_____

Supervisor _____

19 _____ to _____ Position and title _____

Employer _____ Location _____

Accomplishments _____

_____

_____

_____

Supervisor _____

19 _____ to _____ Position and title _____

Employer _____ Location _____

Accomplishments _____

_____

_____

_____

Supervisor _____

19 _____ to _____ Position and title _____

Employer _____ Location _____

Accomplishments _____

_____

_____

_____

Supervisor _____

Honors, Awards, Professional Societies, etc.

List all of the above.

_____

_____

_____

_____

_____

What Else?

List any other *factual* information that demonstrates your skills, abilities, interests, accomplishments, or achievements.

_____

_____

_____

_____

_____

References

Be prepared to have on hand the names and addresses of at least five people (professional preferred) who will give you a good reference. (This will not be printed on your resume, but you will need it.)

Step 4: Writing Your Resume

Now it's time to pull it all together—all of the self-analysis, job targeting, writing practice, and factual inventory, into your own perfect resume, designed to stimulate employer interest and enthusiasm.

You will probably want to have a different version of your resume to cover each major area of employment search or job target. If you have two or three job targets, and they are in the same general work field, and you are using the chronological or functional format, then one version will suffice. If your job targets are reasonably diverse, then you will probably want one version for each target. If you are using the targeted resume, then you get maximum penetration by having a different resume for each target or work title.

In this part of the book we have provided work sheets, examples, and writing guides for each resume format. You need only concern yourself with those pages which relate to your own selected format. Turn to that section now.

PREPARING THE CHRONOLOGICAL RESUME

You have chosen the chronological resume to highlight a good work history related directly to your next job target, without major gaps or numerous job changes.

Rules for the Chronological Resume

1. Start with present or most recent position and work backward, with most space devoted to recent employment.

2. Detail only the last four or five positions, or employment covering the last ten or so years. Summarize early positions unless exceptionally relevant to the present.

3. Use year designations, not month and day. Greater detail can be given in the interview or application.

4. You don't need to show every major position change with a given employer. List the most recent or present and two or three others at the most.

5. Do not repeat details that are common to several positions.

6. Within each position listed stress the *major* accomplishments and responsibilities that demonstrate your full competency to do the job. Once the most significant aspects of your work are clear, it is generally not necessary to include lesser achievements, as they will be assumed by employers.

7. Keep your next job target in mind, and as you describe prior positions and accomplishments emphasize those which are most related to your next move-up.

8. Education is not included in chronological order. If it is within the past five years, it should go at the top of the resume. If earlier than that, at the bottom. (This is not a hard and fast rule, however, and you can follow your own instincts whether to emphasize work or education.)

9. And, of course, keep it to one page.

Employment Counselor

MARSHA M. GRANT
198 Francis Ave.
Oklahoma City, Oklahoma 73109
405-824-6858

Chronological

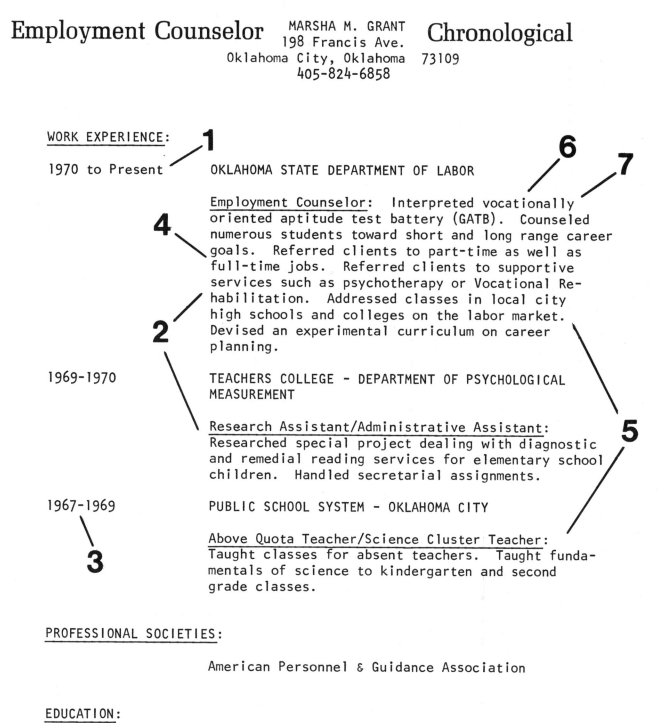

WORK EXPERIENCE: **1**

6   **7**

1970 to Present   OKLAHOMA STATE DEPARTMENT OF LABOR

4

Employment Counselor: Interpreted vocationally
oriented aptitude test battery (GATB). Counseled
numerous students toward short and long range career
goals. Referred clients to part-time as well as
full-time jobs. Referred clients to supportive
services such as psychotherapy or Vocational Rehabilitation. Addressed classes in local city
high schools and colleges on the labor market.
Devised an experimental curriculum on career
planning.

2

1969-1970   TEACHERS COLLEGE - DEPARTMENT OF PSYCHOLOGICAL
                        MEASUREMENT

Research Assistant/Administrative Assistant:
Researched special project dealing with diagnostic
and remedial reading services for elementary school
children. Handled secretarial assignments.

5

1967-1969   PUBLIC SCHOOL SYSTEM - OKLAHOMA CITY

Above Quota Teacher/Science Cluster Teacher:
Taught classes for absent teachers. Taught fundamentals of science to kindergarten and second
grade classes.

3

PROFESSIONAL SOCIETIES:

American Personnel & Guidance Association

EDUCATION:

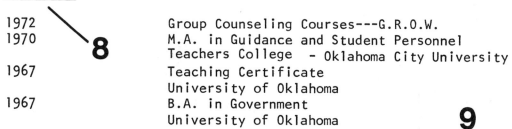

1972   Group Counseling Courses---G.R.O.W.
1970   M.A. in Guidance and Student Personnel
              Teachers College - Oklahoma City University

8

1967   Teaching Certificate
              University of Oklahoma
1967   B.A. in Government
              University of Oklahoma   **9**

Chronological Resume Drafting Forms

INSTRUCTIONS

On the pages that follow, we have provided drafting forms that can be used to prepare your chronological resume. There are two such forms, each of which can be used to condense information relevant to a particular position or employer.

First, look over your resume inventory on pages 79–84 and select those positions you wish to include in your resume. Write these in the spaces provided below. Try to keep to five or fewer past positions in your resume.

Starting with the most recent position on the top of the drafting form, list everything you can think of relating to that job which you accomplished (check pages 82–83 for some reminders). Keep working until you have *filled* the top section with job related results you have produced. Do this with each position you have selected. Then, look over all of the information on the top of the sheets and underline, or highlight, the activities in each position which you feel are most indicative of your abilities and most related to the next step in your career.

In the space at the bottom of the drafting form, rewrite the information you have underscored into a concise and well-written paragraph or two that can be used in your resume.

For example, here is a paragraph as it appears *before* and *after:*

BEFORE:

I started up and then qualified eight beverage and conversion presses at numerous customers' plants that brought in a total revenue of eight million dollars. In addition, I evaluated and hired many machinists and tool and die makers during that two-year period.

AFTER:

Started and qualified eight beverage and conversion presses at various customer plants at a value of $8.0 million. Evaluated and hired numerous machinists and tool and die makers.

Chronological Resume Drafting Form (Sample)

Dates _1977_ to _Present_ Position _Collection Clerk_ _____

Employer _Harrison's Music Publishers, Inc._ _____

In the space below list as many accomplishments or results you can think of which describe your performance in the above position.

I called our customers to collect the unpaid bills they owed us. I invented some form letters to send to our customers asking them to pay their bills. I wrote up the daily remittance report to give to the controller. Helped to settle disputes our customers had about faulty merchandise. I changed our filing system to make it easier to find things in a hurry.

Underline the activities above which you feel are most pertinent to your next job target, and rewrite in condensed form suitable for your resume below.

Collected $1.0 million in receivables in one year. Developed form letters which resulted in more efficient cash flow. Responsible for daily remittance report. Settled customer disputes. Reported directly to corporate controller. Reorganized filing system resulting in quick access to all departmental information.

Chronological Resume Drafting Form No. 1

Dates _____ to _____ Position _____

Employer _____

In the space below list as many accomplishments or results you can think of which describe your performance in the above position.

_____

_____

_____

_____

_____

_____

_____

_____

_____

_____

Underline the activities above which you feel are most pertinent to your next job target, and rewrite in condensed form suitable for your resume below.

_____

_____

_____

_____

_____

_____

Chronological Resume Drafting Form No. 2

Dates _____ to _____ Position _____

Employer _____

In the space below list as many accomplishments or results you can think of which describe your performance in the above position.

_____

_____

_____

_____

_____

_____

_____

_____

_____

_____

Underline the activities above which you feel are most pertinent to your next job target, and rewrite in condensed form suitable for your resume below.

_____

_____

_____

_____

_____

_____

Note: Make additional copies of this form as necessary.

Final Assembly of Your Chronological Resume

You have now completed all of the informational development for your resume. What remains is to simply assemble it into a finished draft. Follow these easy steps:

1. Review the various chronological layouts in the sample resumes section. Decide which layout appeals to you most and follow this.

2. Start with a fresh sheet of paper and list name, address, zip code, and phone number (with area code). If your education is within the past five years, put it next after your address block. If previously, include it at the bottom.

3. Transcribe the date/position employer information and the condensed paragraphs from the bottom of each of the resume drafting forms you have just completed.

4. When you have assembled all information on the first draft, check it over very carefully for omissions, irrelevancies, inaccuracies, and length. Make whatever corrections or additions you feel to be required for the strongest personal presentation of yourself on one page.

5. Have a second draft typed from the first—incorporating all changes. This is the copy that you will present to others for evaluating and editing, and it should be very close to the way you would like your final perfect resume to look. Cut it back as necessary to fit one page (see pages 72–77 for tips on fitting on one page).

6. Final Critique—This is the last step before the final typing and printing—the final sign-off of a most important document. Decide upon someone you feel has a very good grasp of spelling, grammar, and punctuation and is willing to provide you with critical feedback. Give this person a copy of your final draft and ask

Chronological Resume Checklist

YES | NO

_____|_____ * Are there any typing or spelling errors? (check twice)

_____|_____ * Are all statements easily understood?

_____|_____ * Is writing style concise and direct?

_____|_____ * Are paragraphs and sentences short and to the point?

_____|_____ * Have redundancies and repetitions been eliminated?

_____|_____ * Does each position demonstrate easily understood accomplishments?

_____|_____ * Are all major relevant time periods covered?

_____|_____ * Has all unnecessary information been eliminated?

_____|_____ * Is layout simple, professional and attractive?

_____|_____ * Does resume present best possible picture of candidate?

him/her to go over it with you, and point out any areas where it can be improved. Use the checklist on the facing page as a guide:

Assuming you have passed (or corrected) all of the checklisted items, it's all downhill from now. Turn to pages 128–132 to learn about final typing and printing, and then valuable information about cover letters.

PREPARING THE FUNCTIONAL RESUME

By selecting the Functional Resume format, you have chosen to highlight your basic area of ability and potential rather than your work history. In doing this you will be able to organize and highlight information in a particular career target direction, and play down possible gaps or inconsistencies in past work. If you are changing careers, entering or re-entering the job market, you have chosen an approach that will also allow you to easily talk about non-paying work experience and school or community activities.

Rules for the Functional Resume

1. Use four or five separate paragraphs, each one headlining a particular area of expertise or involvement.

2. List the functional paragraphs in order of importance with the area most related to your present job target at the top and containing slightly more information.

3. Within each functional area stress the most directly related accomplishments or results you have produced or the most powerful abilities (see pages 48–49).

4. Know that you can include any relevant accomplishment without necessarily identifying which employer or non-employment situation it was connected to.

5. Include education toward the bottom, unless it was within the past three years. If it was in an unrelated field, include it at the end regardless of how recent.

6. List a brief synopsis of your actual work experience at the bottom, giving dates, employer, and title. If you have had no work experience or a very spotty record, leave out the employment synopsis entirely (but be prepared to talk about the subject at the interview).

7. And keep the length to one page.

Design Engineer   STAN MARLEY WATSON   Functional

6750 Peachtree Industrial Blvd., Apt. D-2
Atlanta, Georgia 30360   (404) 556-1270

DESIGN ENGINEERING ——**2**

Planned and organized technical development projects on process equipment such as dryers, vessel components and product coolers.

Created technical standards and design methods for subsidiary of American Can Company. Designed forms, drawing and specification formats and developed procedures for implementing these methods.

3

Wrote technical paper on use of goliath cranes in shipbuilding for the Society of Naval Architects and Marine Engineers. These cranes now used nationwide.

1

Designed plant piping systems, HVAC for industrial buildings, gas storage facilities, and overhead crane lifting equipment for shipbuilding subsidiary of Tenneco, Inc.

SUPERVISION AND MANAGEMENT

Supervised engineers and draftsmen in the design of process equipment and the writing of specifications for resource recovery plants.

Resolved field problems associated with equipment start-up. Coordinated efforts of owners and contractors. Determined and recommended modifications of equipment.

FINANCIAL PLANNING AND DEVELOPMENT

Developed customer proposals and plant layouts. Created entire financial picture which included product value as well as costs--from raw materials and operations through marketing and administration.

Prepared specifications, evaluated bids, and inspected construction of over $40 million in manufacturing equipment for a new shipyard.

4

PROFESSIONAL STANDING

Registered Professional Engineer, States of Virginia and Georgia.

EDUCATION AND EXPERIENCE ——**5**

6

1977 - 79	M.B.A. in Management--University of Georgia
1977 - 78	Air-Tech Corporation--Senior Design Engineer
1971 - 77	Newport Shipbuilding--Design Engineer
	Associate Design Engineer
1967 - 71	B.S. in Mechanical Engineering--Va. Poly. Institute

7

Sample List of Functional Headings

Check off the functions below that best describe your abilities and potential and are in line with your job target. Add any others that are appropriate. Narrow the list to four or five top choices and use these on your functional resume.

Management	Construction	Promotion
Advertising	Culinary	Investment
Secretarial	Boating	Drafting
Administrative	Aviation	Graphic design
Public relations	Supervision	Printing
Accounting	Organization	Layout
Communication	Purchasing	Materials handling
Design	Acquisition	Market research
Engineering	Planning	Instruction
Retailing	Scheduling	Construction
Selling	Career development	Programming
Writing and editing	Employment	Presentations
Research	Interviewing	Production
Finance	Public speaking	Investigation
Real estate	Fund raising	Architecture
Counseling	Community affairs	Program development
Medicine	Teaching	Chemistry
Legal	Systems and procedures	Social work
Electronics	Product development	Navigation
Data processing	Testing	
Publicity	Inspecting	

Additional functions not included in our list:

_____   _____

_____   _____

_____   _____

_____   _____

Functional Resume Drafting Forms

INSTRUCTIONS

On the following pages we have provided three special forms with which to draft your functional resume. Use them as noted.

Start by reviewing the information on pages 48 and 49 and reacquaint yourself with the earlier description of your capabilities. Then, go over the sample list of functional categories above, checking off and adding any that you feel represent major areas of your capability or potential and are also related to your job target.

Narrow the list to the five most powerful functions, and list them in order of relevance, on the tops of the forms that follow. On the top segment of the form write down everything you can think of that represents an ability, achievement, or accomplishment from any prior experience or position—paid or unpaid—within that functional area. List as much as you need to fill the space.

Underline or highlight the most important or relevant items in the top segment. In the lower space of the form, rewrite the paragraph, communicating clearly and concisely the most important elements you have underlined.

Here is an example of a *before* and *after* paragraph.

BEFORE:

I helped to put together and completely organize a small mail order book company. I also surveyed and then recommended potential markets. I set up a functional marketing file for the regional sales office. I prepared various market research studies.

AFTER:

Established and organized mail order book company. Analyzed and developed potential markets. Created functional marketing file for regional sales office. Prepared efficient market research study successfully used over 18 month period.

Functional Resume Drafting Form (Sample)

Function title: _Social Services_

In the space below, write down all achievements, accomplishments, or results *of any kind* that you have produced in your work experience, non-work experience, school or community activities. Don't go below the dotted line. (You can review pages 41 to 46 for ideas.)

I led a group of Senior Girl Scouts on a summer "outward bound" adventure tour. I taught them food survival in the wilderness. I trained a group of 12 senior citizens in the craft of macramé. I visited prisons and taught team sports to women prisoners. The basketball team that I trained won first place among six other teams for the winter season. As a hospital volunteer I advised people on good nutrition and assisted three women in breaking the smoking habit. One of these women has not touched a cigarette in 4 1/2 years.

Go over what you have written above, underline or highlight the most relevant information, and condense in the space provided a concise, effective resume paragraph.

Trained groups of all ages in crafts and sports participation. Led 18 teenagers through successful survival course. Instructed incarcerated women in team support and spirit that resulted in first place win among six other teams. Aided women in breaking through minor drug dependency.

Functional Resume Drafting Form No. 1

Function title: _____

In the space below, write down all achievements, accomplishments, or results *of any kind* that you have produced in your work experience, non-work experience, school or community activities. Don't go below the dotted line. (You can review pages 41 to 46 for ideas.)

_____

_____

_____

_____

_____

_____

_____

_____

. . . .

Go over what you have written above, underline or highlight the most relevant information, and condense in the space provided a concise, effective resume paragraph. (See writing rules on pages 72–77.)

_____

_____

_____

_____

_____

Functional Resume Drafting Form No. 2

Function title: _____

In the space below, write down all achievements, accomplishments, or results *of any kind* that you have produced in your work experience, non-work experience, school or community activities. Don't go below the dotted line. (You can review pages 41 to 46 for ideas.)

_____

_____

_____

_____

_____

_____

_____

_____

. . . .

Go over what you have written above, underline or highlight the most relevant information, and condense in the space provided a concise, effective resume paragraph. (See writing rules on pages 72–77.)

_____

_____

_____

_____

_____

Functional Resume Drafting Form No. 3

Function title: _____

In the space below, write down all achievements, accomplishments, or results *of any kind* that you have produced in your work experience, non-work experience, school or community activities. Don't go below the dotted line. (You can review pages 41 to 46 for ideas.)

_____

_____

_____

_____

_____

_____

_____

_____

. . . .

Go over what you have written above, underline or highlight the most relevant information, and condense in the space provided a concise, effective resume paragraph. (See writing rules on pages 72–77.)

_____

_____

_____

_____

_____

Note: Make additional copies of this form as necessary.

Final Assembly of Your Functional Resume

You have completed all of the information development of your functional resume. What remains is to pull it all together into a one-page masterpiece. The steps are simple:

1. Review the functional layouts in the sample resumes section and pick the one that appeals to you most. Use this as a guide.

2. Start with name, address, zip code, phone with area code. If your last completed education was less than five years ago, include it at the top. If over five years ago include it at the bottom. (This is not a hard and fast rule, and you can emphasize or de-emphasize education as you wish.)

3. Transcribe the functional headings and condensed paragraphs from the resume drafting forms you have just completed. If you are doing the draft by hand or typing double space, use two pieces of paper attached end to end to see how much you will need to condense to end up with one page.

4. After the functional descriptions add a *brief* chronology of employment unless you feel that this would not be in your best interest.

5. Have a second draft typed from the first, incorporating all changes. This is the copy that you will present to others for evaluation and critique and should be very close to the way you would like your final perfect resume to look. Cut it back as necessary to fit one page (see pages 72–77 for tips on fitting into one page).

6. Final Critique—This is the last step before the final typing and printing—the final sign-off of a most important document. Identify someone you feel has a very good grasp of basic grammar, spelling, and punctuation and is willing to pro-

Functional Resume Checklist

YES | NO

_____|_____ * Are there any typing or spelling errors? (check twice)

_____|_____ * Are all statements easily understood?

_____|_____ * Is writing style concise and direct?

_____|_____ * Are paragraphs and sentences short and to the point?

_____|_____ * Have redundancies and repetitions been eliminated?

_____|_____ * Does each position demonstrate easily understood accomplishments?

_____|_____ * Are all major relevant time periods covered?

_____|_____ * Has all unnecessary information been eliminated?

_____|_____ * Is layout simple, professional and attractive?

_____|_____ * Does resume present best possible picture of candidate?

vide you with critical feedback. Give that person a copy of your final draft and ask him/her to go over it with you, and point out any places where it can be improved. Use the checklist on the facing page as a guide:

Assuming you have passed (or corrected) all of the checklisted items, it's all downhill now. Turn to pages 128–132 to learn about final typing and printing, and then some valuable information about cover letters.

PREPARING THE TARGETED RESUME

With this book, we are introducing a brand new resume format designed to focus your capabilities and accomplishments sharply toward a well-developed job target. Unlike the chronological and functional resumes, which are geared toward an affirmative picture of past history, the targeted resume features a series of statements concerning what **you can do—your capabilities,** whether or not you have actually had directly relevant experience.

You are using the targeted resume because you are clear about a particular job target or targets (use a different resume for each) and your willingness to focus on these alone. The resume is actually quite simple to prepare, so it would not be difficult to put together two or three different ones.

Rules for the Targeted Resume

1. You must be clear about a specific job target (or targets if you plan several versions). A job target is a clear description of a particular title or occupational field that you want to pursue (see page 60 and those preceding).

2. The statements of capability and accomplishment must all be directly related to the job target. This may require some reading or research in the field.

3. Both capabilities and accomplishments will be short statements of one or two lines, generally written in an active style.

4. Listed capabilities will answer the underlying question *"What can you do?"* Listed accomplishments will answer the underlying question *"What have you done?"*

5. Experience and education are listed but not openly stressed—they support rather than control.

6. The resume should easily fit on one page with plenty of "white space."

Senior Credit Analyst   FRANK CARIOU   Targeted

22 Mayhew Road
Bloomfield, New Jersey 07001
201-746-3730

1

JOB TARGET: SENIOR CREDIT ANALYST IN A MULTIMILLION DOLLAR
ENGINEERING DIVISION OF A MAJOR BLUE CHIP CORPORATION

CAPABILITIES:

* Analyze credit data to estimate degree of risk ——**3**
* Prepare reports of credit data findings
* Contact banks, trade and credit associations, salespeople and others to obtain credit information
* Study and report on economic trends in a firm's industry
  or branch of industry to predict probable success of new
  customer
* Visit establishments to determine condition of plant and
  equipment. Compare methods of operation with accepted
  practices in industry
* Evaluate results of investigations; prepare reports of
  findings; suggest credit limitations to management
* Consult with management to assist with corporate planning

4

2 ACHIEVEMENTS:

* Responsible for ten million dollars in receivables for the
  Chemical Division of a major blue chip corporation.
* Acted as company consultant on general economic development
  and trends with responsibilities for speaking on the subject
  at sales and customer counseling sessions.
* Supervised a staff of eight in a two million dollar branch of
  a large credit corporation--staff included a collection manager
  and a credit supervisor.
* Maintained complete autonomy in profit and loss management
  within same branch.
* Handled R.O.I. and present value analysis of investment and
  capital proposals.
* Acted as Credit Manager for three month period in Canadian
  branch of blue chip corporation.

WORK HISTORY:

1973-Present	G.A.F. Corporation	Senior Credit Analyst
1972-1973	General Electric Credit Corp.	Credit & Collection Manager
1966-1969	Great Western Insurance	Claims Examiner

EDUCATION:

6

1975	**5**—Pace University	M.B.A. in Finance
1972	C.C.N.Y.	B.S. in Accounting

Writing Your Targeted Resume

• Preparing a targeted resume is actually an easy process, since the substantive material essentially comes out of the answers to two basic questions about your job target(s): *What can you do?* and *What have you done?*

• Using the forms that follow, you will create fifteen to twenty statements of capability and of accomplishment for each target, and then boil these down to the most powerful.

• Start by writing down one, two, or three specific job targets below. They can be from the earlier pages of this book, or you can come up with others.

Job Target No. 1 _____

Job Target No. 2 _____

Job Target No. 3 _____

We have provided enough work sheets for you to produce these resumes.

• For each job target, complete one *capabilities work sheet* and one *accomplishments work sheet,* and combine them in accordance with the sample format shown.

Capabilities Work Sheet

(WHAT YOU *CAN* DO)

Sample Job Target: _____

Repeat each question to yourself and fill in the answer denoting what you *feel* or *think* that you can do (whether or not you have done it) or could do in the performance of that job target. Continue to ask these questions until you have a list of at least twenty answers. Then select or rewrite the most powerful ten.

Q.   As regards you job target, what can you do?

A.   I can *put people at ease.*

Q.   As regards your job target, list something else you can do.

A.   I can *ask direct questions without embarrassment.*

Q.   As regards your job target, what else can you do?

A.   I can *offer compassion and sympathy to others.*

Q.   In relation to your job target, list something you can do.

A.   I can *read and interpret insurance policies.*

Q.   What else is there that you can do related to your job target?

A.   I can *remember lots of people's names without faltering.*

Q. As regards your job target, what can you do that creates value?

A. I can *judge potential talent.*

Q. As regards your job target, what can you do that relates to money?

A. I can *be shrewd about salary negotiating.*

Q. Regarding your job target, think of something else you can do.

A. I can *hide any personal upsets that could get in the way.*

Q. Regarding your job target, what could you do if you were willing to play 100 percent?

A. I could *fire an ineffective staff with no upset or guilt.*

Q. As regards your job target, what can you do that produces value for people?

A. I can *interpret people's underlying fears.*

Q. List something else you can do that would be related to your job target.

A. I can *inspire and motivate people.*

Q. What would you be willing to do about your job target that would be valuable?

A. I can *correct people without offending them.*

Q. What can you do in another field that could be related to your job target?

A. I can *write detailed and informative reports.*

Q. What else can you do that could be valuable in your job target objective?

A. I can *take a lot of pressure.*

Q. What can you do in your non-work life that could be applicable to your job target?

A. I can *organize teams for sports or play.*

Q. What other things can you do or could do that would be valuable in your job target?

A. I can *support people with big egos.*

A. I could *make high-level, difficult decisions about people.*

A. I can *create new job functions.*

A. I could *rearrange an entire organizational structure.*

Don't stop this process until you have come up with at least twenty *I cans* or *I coulds*. Remember that these don't need to be things you *have* done, just tasks that you feel confident you can or could do that would be valuable in your job target. Go over your list and put an X in front of ten of the capabilities you would like to include in your resume. And then complete the accomplishments work sheet.

Accomplishments Work Sheet

(WHAT YOU *HAVE* DONE)

Sample Job Target _____

Read and answer each question with a short statement describing something tangible you have *done*. What results or accomplishments *from any area of your experience—work or non-work*—that will illustrate or demonstrate your ability to produce results in your job target area. Continue to answer the questions until you have come up with at least twelve to fifteen "I haves," which can be reduced to eight for your resume.

Q.   As regards your job target, what have you done?

A.   I have *assisted over 300 people in rewriting their resumes.*

Q.   As regards your job target, what else have you done?

A.   I have *hired regular and auxiliary staff for a small company*

Q.   As regards your job target, what else have you done?

A.   I have *trained in numerous motivational programs.*

Q.   What is something else you have done that relates to your job target?

A.   I have *fired accountants, lawyers, and regular staff.*

Q.   As regards your job target, what result have you produced?

A.   I have *assisted line managers in the firing process.*

Q.   As regards your job target, what have you accomplished?

A.   I have *directed and advised numerous people into new careers.*

Q.   As regards your job target, list something you have achieved.

A.   I have *trained many individuals in effective interviewing technique*

Q.   Regarding your job target, list something you have done in another field that could be related.

A.   I have *directed two women in starting successful fashion consulting busine*

Q. Regarding your job target, list something you have done that you are proud of.

A. I have *intervened for impoverished people during emotional crises.*

Q. Regarding your job target, what have you done that was valuable financially to someone else?

A. I have *trained a man to negotiate for and obtain a 40 percent salary increase.*

Q. Regarding your job target, think of something tangible you have done.

A. I have *read over 1000 resumes.*

Q. Identify something you have done in your private life that relates to your job target.

A. I have *supported others to be straightforward in communicating.*

Q. Regarding your job target, what have you done that demonstrates an ability to work with people?

A. I have *supervised six caseworkers who were responsible for 400 people.*

Q. Think of some other things you have done in work or non-work-related experiences that demonstrate your ability to produce results?

A. I have *trained and developed career counselors.*

A. I have *sold counseling services to major corporations.*

A. I have *led career day seminars on college campuses.*

A. I have *entertained hundreds of people as a singer.*

Go back over all of the "I haves" you have listed and select eight of these for actual use in your resume. Put an X in front of each of these.

Capabilities Work Sheet

(WHAT YOU *CAN* DO)

Job Target No. 1 _____

Repeat each question to yourself and fill in the answer denoting what you *feel* or *think* that you can do (whether or not you have done it) or could do in the performance of that job target. Continue to ask these questions until you are satisfied that you have a full list of at least twenty answers. Then select or rewrite the most powerful ten.

Q. As regards your job target, what can you do?

A. I can _____

Q.   As regards your job target, list something else you can do.

A.   I can _____

Q.   As regards your job target, what else can you do?

A.   I can _____

Q.   In relation to your job target, list something you can do.

A.   I can _____

Q.   What else is there that you can do related to your job target?

A.   I can _____

Q.   As regards your job target, what can you do that creates value?

A.   I can _____

Q.   As regards your job target, what can you do that relates to money?

A.   I can _____

Q.   Regarding your job target, think of something else you can do.

A.   I can _____

Q.   Regarding your job target, what could you do if you were willing to play 100 percent?

A.   I could _____

Q.   As regards your job target, what can you do that produces value for people?

A.   I can _____

Q.   List something else you can do that would be related to your job target.

A.   I can _____

Q.   What would you be willing to do regarding your job target that would be valuable?

A.   I would be willing to _____

Q.   What can you do in another field that could be related to your job target?

A.   I can _____

Q.   What else can you do that could be valuable in your job target objective?

A.   I can _____

Q. What can you do in your non-work life that could be applicable to your job target?

A. I can _____

Q. What other things can you do or could do that would be valuable in your job target?

A. I can _____

A. I could _____

A. I can _____

A. I could _____

Don't stop this process until you have come up with at least twenty *I cans* or *I coulds*. Remember that these don't need to be things you *have* done, just tasks that you feel confident you can or could do that would be valuable in your job target. Go over your list and put an X in front of ten of the capabilities you would like to include in your resume. And then complete the accomplishments work sheet. See page 120 for assembling instructions.

Accomplishments Work Sheet

(WHAT YOU *HAVE* DONE)

Job Target No. 1 _____
Read and answer each question with a short statement describing something tangible you have *done*. What results or accomplishments *from any area of your experience—work or non-work—*that will illustrate or demonstrate your ability to produce results in your job target area. Continue to answer the questions until you have come up with at least twelve to fifteen "I haves," which can be reduced to eight for your resume.

Q. As regards your job target, what have you done?

A. I have _____

Q. As regards your job target, what else have you done?

A. I have _____

Q. As regards your job target, what else have you done?

A. I have _____

Q. What is something else you have done that relates to your job target?

A. I have _____

Q.   As regards your job target, what result have you produced?

A.   I have _____

Q.   As regards your job target, what have you accomplished?

A.   I have _____

Q.   Regarding your job target, list something you have done in another field that could be related.

A.   I have _____

Q.   Regarding your job target, list something you have done that you are proud of.

A.   I have _____

Q.   Regarding your job target, what have you done that was valuable financially to someone else?

A.   I have _____

Q.   Regarding your job target, think of something tangible you have done.

A.   I have _____

Q.   Identify something you have done in your private life that relates to your job target.

A.   I have _____

Q.   Regarding your job target, what have you done that demonstrates an ability to work with people?

A.   I have _____

Q.   Think of some other things you have done in work or non-work-related experiences that demonstrate your ability to produce results?

A.   I have _____

A.   I have _____

A.   I have _____

A.   I have _____

Go back over all of the "I haves" you have listed and select eight of these for actual use in your resume. Put an X in front of these.

Capabilities Work Sheet

(WHAT YOU *CAN* DO)

Job Target No. 2 _____

Repeat each question to yourself and fill in the answer denoting what you *feel* or *think* that you can do (whether or not you have done it) or could do in the performance of that job target. Continue to ask these questions until you are satisfied that you have a full list of at least twenty. Then select or rewrite the most powerful ten.

Q. As regards your job target, what can you do?

A. I can _____

Q. As regards your job target, list something else you can do.

A. I can _____

Q. As regards your job target, what else can you do?

A. I can _____

Q. In relation to your job target, list something you can do.

A. I can _____

Q. What else is there that you can do related to your job target?

A. I can _____

Q. As regards your job target, what can you do that creates value?

A. I can _____

Q. As regards your job target, what can you do that relates to money?

A. I can _____

Q. Regarding your job target, think of something else you can do.

A. I can _____

Q. Regarding your job target, what could you do if you were willing to play 100 percent?

A. I could _____

Q. As regards your job target, what can you do that produces value for people?

A. I can _____

Q. List something else you can do that would be related to your job target.

A. I can _____

Q. What would you be willing to do about your job target that would be valuable?

A. I would be willing to _____

Q. What can you do in another field that could be related to your job target?

A. I can _____

Q. What else can you do that could be valuable in your job target objective?

A. I can _____

Q. What can you do in your non-work life that could be applicable to your job target?

A. I can _____

Q. What other things can you do or could do that would be valuable in your job target?

A. I can _____

A. I could _____

A. I can _____

A. I could _____

Don't stop this process until you have come up with at least twenty *I cans* or *I coulds*. Remember that these don't need to be things you *have* done, just tasks that you feel confident you can or could do that would be valuable in your job target. Go over your list and put an X in front of ten of the capabilities you would like to include in your resume. And then complete the accomplishments work sheet.

Accomplishments Work Sheet

(WHAT YOU *HAVE* DONE)

Job Target No. 2 _____

Read and answer each question with a short statement describing something tangible you have *done*. What results or accomplishments *from any area of your experience—work or non-work—*that will illustrate or demonstrate your ability to produce results in your job target area. Continue to answer the questions until you have come up with at least twelve to fifteen "I haves," which can be reduced to eight for your resume.

Q. As regards your job target, what have you done?

A. I have _____

Q. As regards your job target, what else have you done?

A. I have _____

Q. As regards your job target, what else have you done?

A. I have _____

Q. What is something else you have done that relates to your job target?

A. I have _____

Q. As regards your job target, what result have you produced?

A. I have _____

Q. As regards your job target, what have you accomplished?

A. I have _____

Q. As regards your job target, list something you have achieved.

A. I have _____

Q. Regarding your job target, list something you have done in another field that could be related.

A. I have _____

Q. Regarding your job target, list something you have done that you are proud of.

A. I have _____

Q. Regarding your job target, what have you done that was valuable financially to someone else?

A. I have _____

Q. Regarding your job target, think of something tangible you have done.

A. I have _____

Q. Identify something you have done in your private life that relates to your job target.

A. I have _____

Q. Regarding your job target, what have you done that demonstrates an ability to work with people?

A. I have _____

Q. Think of some other things you have done in work or non-work-related experiences that demonstrate your ability to produce results?

A. I have _____

A. I have _____

A. I have _____

A. I have _____

Go back over all of the "I haves" you have listed and select eight of these for actual use in your resume. Put an X in front of each of these.

Capabilities Work Sheet

(WHAT YOU *CAN* DO)

Job Target No. 3 _____
Repeat each question to yourself and fill in the answer denoting what you *feel* or *think* that you can do (whether or not you have done it) or could do in the performance of that job target. Continue to ask these questions until you are satisfied that you have a full list of at least twenty. Then select or rewrite the most powerful ten.

Q. As regards your job target, what can you do?

A. I can _____

Q. As regards your job target, list something else you can do.

A. I can _____

Q. As regards your job target, what else can you do?

A. I can _____

Q. In relation to your job target, list something you can do.

A. I can _____

Q. What else is there that you can do related to your job target?

A. I can _____

Q. As regards your job target, what can you do that creates value?

A. I can _____

Q. As regards your job target, what can you do that relates to money?

A. I can _____

Q. Regarding your job target, think of something else you can do.

A. I can _____

Q. Regarding your job target, what could you do if you were willing to play 100 percent?

A. I could _____

Q. As regards your job target, what can you do that produces value for people?

A. I can _____

Q. List something else you can do that would be related to your job target.

A. I can _____

Q. What would you be willing to do regarding your job target that would be valuable?

A. I would be willing to _____

Q. What can you do in another field that could be related to your job target?

A. I can _____

Q. What else can you do that could be valuable in your job target objective?

A. I can _____

Q. What can you do in your non-work life that could be applicable to your job target?

A. I can _____

Q. What other things can you do or could do that would be valuable in your job target?

A. I can _____

A. I could _____

A. I can _____

A. I could _____

Don't stop this process until you have come up with at least twenty *I cans* or *I coulds*. Remember that these don't need to be things you *have* done, just tasks that you feel confident you can or could do that would be valuable in your job target. Go over your list and put an X in front of ten of the capabilities you would like to include in your resume. And then complete the accomplishments work sheet.

Accomplishments Work Sheet

(WHAT YOU *HAVE* DONE)

Job Target No. 3 _____

Read and answer each question with a short statement describing something tangible you have *done*. What results or accomplishments *from any area of your experience—work or non-work*—that will illustrate or demonstrate your ability to produce results in your job target area. Continue to answer the questions until you have come up with at least twelve to fifteen "I haves," which can be reduced to eight for your resume.

Q. As regards your job target, what have you done?

A. I have _____

Q. As regards your job target, what else have you done?

A. I have _____

Q. As regards your job target, what else have you done?

A. I have _____

Q. What is something else you have done that relates to your job target?

A. I have _____

Q. As regards your job target, what result have you produced?

A. I have _____

Q. As regards your job target, what have you accomplished?

A. I have _____

Q. As regards your job target, list something you have achieved.

A. I have _____

Q. Regarding your job target, list something you have done in another field that could be related.

A. I have _____

Q. Regarding your job target, list something you have done that you are proud of.

A. I have _____

Q. Regarding your job target what have you done that was valuable financially to someone else?

    A. I have _____

Q. Regarding your job target, think of something tangible you have done.

    A. I have _____

Q. Identify something you have done in your private life that relates to your job target.

    A. I have _____

Q. Regarding your job target, what have you done that demonstrates an ability to work with people?

    A. I have _____

Q. Think of some other things you have done in work or non-work-related experiences that demonstrate your ability to produce results?

    A. I have _____

    A. I have _____

    A. I have _____

    A. I have _____

Go back over all of the "I haves" you have listed and select eight of these for actual use in your resume. Put an X in front of each of these.

Final Assembly of Your Targeted Resume

As you will see from the resume samples at the back of the book (see pages 154–194), layouts for the Targeted Resume are all essentially the same. The format has been designed for simplicity and directness.

Your job target is at the top, after your name, address, and phone, with your *Capabilities* right under it describing what you *can do* in that target, followed by your *Accomplishments*, which illustrate what you *have done*—thus supporting your capabilities, followed by your actual work *Experience*, which gives you additional credibility. Your *Education* comes at the end.

The assembly of your resume is therefore quite easy.

1. Start by listing name, address, zip code, and phone number (with area code).

2. List your specific job target next in all capital letters or by capitalizing the initial letter of each word.

3. Set aside the heading *Capabilities* as shown. If you like, you may follow this with a sentence such as:

In my job target area I am able to achieve the following: _____

4. Then list ten to twelve brief capabilities statements selected from the appropriate work sheet, starring each of these with a (•) or (*) or (_) for emphasis and style.

5. Follow this with the heading *Accomplishments.* (If you wish, you may also include a lead-in statement such as:

Listed below are some of the ac- *complishments related to my job target:* _____).

6. Then list six to eight accomplishments from the appropriate work sheet in concise statements preceded by (•) or (*) or (_) for emphasis and style.

7. Follow this with the heading *Experience,* and use no more than five lines to summarize your work history (dates, employer, title). If you have more positions to list than five lines will allow, it is all right to combine earlier jobs in a statement such as:

1965–70 Held other commercial positions.

8. This is followed with the heading *Education.* You should use only two or three lines to detail your most recent education—school, degree or program, dates.

9. When you have all of the information assembled, type a single space draft to fit neatly on one page. If you have more space, you can add other capabilities or accomplishments. If you need to cut back, you can shorten or delete the least needed information. This is your final draft.

10. Have someone you trust go over the resume and critique it for completeness, clarity, spelling, neatness, and organization. Encourage criticism.

11. Make all corrections and adjustments.

You have finished the final draft of your Targeted Resume. If, as we suggest, you have two or three different job targets, you will want to go through the same procedure with your other targets.

For instructions on the final typing and printing, turn to Step 5 on pages 128–132— Typing, Layout, and Printing.

PREPARING THE RESUME ALTERNATIVE

Use this format if you are in a situation where it is really not appropriate to use one of the more traditional resumes. For example, if you have been out of the labor force for a number of years, as a housewife with very few outside activities, or perhaps in a job that is so far removed from your new job target that a resume would appear to disqualify you. More romantically, perhaps you have been on a round-the-world sailing trip, or (less romantically) perhaps recovering from a serious illness.

The resume alternative letter is a personalized communication to an individual potential employer, and reflects a clear communication of what you can do for him/her or the firm in very specific terms. It looks forward, rather than backward, and very clearly and specifically answers the question *Why should I hire you?*

It takes research—lots of it—to help you zero in on the particular activities of an employer that you can contribute to. It also takes thorough introspection and self-analysis (Steps 1 and 2 of this book are invaluable here) to be clear about what you can offer. The idea is to present enough about yourself and your ability to make a contribution to an employer, in unstructured form, so that there is no need for a resume.

Rules for the Resume Alternative Letter

1. Be sure to complete the Career Discovery Process at the beginning of this book as far as you possibly can.

2. Be very specific in choosing your job targets.

3. Identify several specific *employers,* doing enough research (see pages 205–206) so that you know exactly what organizations you would like to get interviews with, and the name of the person you need to meet with (not necessarily personnel) to get an offer of employment.

4. Find out as much as you can about the firms you have targeted so that you can identify areas where you could make a real contribution to an ongoing activity.

5. In your letter, communicate enough basic factual information about yourself so that a full resume is not really needed. Keep to one page.

6. Construct the letter so that a "meeting" with the employer is the next natural step. Suggest a time and place to get together.

7. Make each letter as professional appearing as possible—typed on your own preprinted letterhead stationery and proofread thoroughly.

Administrative Coordinator   Targeted

2832 Rhodes Avenue
St. Louis, Missouri 63109
314-572-3836

Mr. Anthony J. Cowles ——— **3**
Medi-Consult Group
1200 Olive Street Road
Olivette, Missouri 63137

Dear Mr. Cowles:

Dr. Anton Ferrano at Washington University Medical School suggested I
contact you about the studies your firm is currently making into the
utilization of nursing homes in Missouri and Illinois. He also remarked
that you might be thinking about hiring someone to coordinate the field
investigations which are part of your study.

2

As vice-president of our local Woman's Action Community, I have had a
great deal of experience with the operation of day care centers, which,
as you know, are quite similar administratively to nursing homes. My
experience has led me to the financial and administration aspects of
the centers as well as knowledge of the programming and educational
considerations. I have met with the staffs of most of the day care
centers in the county, and am certain that my ability to work with these
professionals would enable me to facilitate the execution of your study.

4

5

In addition to this experience, I have had two years of administrative
work on a timely and significant research project in health care at
Washington University while working on my master's degree in education.

I will be near your office next week and wonder if we could get together
on Wednesday or Thursday for a brief meeting. I'll call you to confirm
when you will be available.

6

Yours truly,

Annette Ebeling-Vorst
Annette Ebeling-Vorst

7

Resume Alternative Letter

DRAFTING FORM #1

Prior to writing each alternative letter, fill out this form after doing as much research as you can (review pages 205 to 206).

EMPLOYER PROSPECT _____

Name of person you want to meet and title _____

Employer _____ Division or dept. _____

Address _____ Phone _____

What is your specific job target with this employer? Describe. _____

_____

_____

What could you do for that employer that would create direct measurable value?

_____

_____

What else could you do? _____

_____

What can you say about *what you have done* that will *demonstrate* your ability to produce results for the employer? _____

_____

Is there anything about your education or training (formal or informal) that you can mention in your letter that will be relevant to what you want to do?

_____

_____

Is there any prior work activity (paid or unpaid) you should mention to demonstrate your fitness for the job target? _____

_____

When would you like to meet with this employer? _____

_____

Is there any other directly relevant information that will help make the employer want to see you? _____

_____

Resume Alternative Letter

DRAFTING FORM #2

Prior to writing each alternative letter, fill out this form, doing whatever research is necessary (review pages 205 to 206).

EMPLOYER PROSPECT _____

Name of person you want to meet and title _____

Employer _____ Division or dept. _____

Address _____ Phone _____

What is your specific job target with this employer? Describe.

_____

_____

What can you do for the employer that would create direct measurable value?

_____

_____

What else can you do? _____

_____

What can you say about *what you have done* that will *demonstrate* your ability to produce results for the employer? _____

_____

Is there anything about your education or training (formal or informal) that you can mention in your letter that will be relevant to what you want to do?

_____

_____

Is there any prior work activity (paid or unpaid) you should mention to demonstrate your fitness for the job target? _____

_____

When would you like to meet with this employer? _____

_____

Is there any other directly relevant information that will help make the employer want to see you? _____

_____

PREPARING THE CREATIVE ALTERNATIVE RESUME

The first rule about the creative alternative is not to take this approach unless you are truly able to put together a level of communication that works creatively in *the eyes of others*—and would be so interpreted by the person it is directed to. Resume readers are a jaded lot, and the line between creativity and gimickry can be very thin to them.

The creative alternative is more of a demonstration than a description of what you can do. Some of the occasions we have seen it used effectively are:

- Advertising copywriter (a well-written ad for oneself)
- Greeting card illustrator (oneself as subject of card)
- Magazine illustrator (cartoon strip about oneself)
- New product manager (a "self as product" description)
- Models (montage of photos—details on back)
- Actor (picture and copies of reviews)
- Fund raiser (letter "soliciting" an interview)

For each one we have seen work there have been ten that have fallen flat. Here are some pointers to consider if this approach appeals to you.

- Consider preparing a more conventional resume as a backup.
- Make sure that what you do is very professionally produced or reproduced.
- Make the results look effortless—not that you had to stay up nights producing it.
- Stay on the side of brevity and simplicity.
- Make sure that the point is made: a personal meeting is called for.

We have not provided any samples of the creative alternatives, since there is, in fact, no pattern to follow.

Step 5: Typing, Layout, and Printing

Before that resume of yours is seriously read by anyone in the employment cycle, it has to pass what we call the *flash test*—that first three- to four-second look in which the reader decides whether or not it's worth reading any further—rather analagous to the way that you yourself might scan pages of a newspaper or magazine to decide which articles or advertisements are worth reading.

Unfortunately, in this unfair employment world of ours, skills just aren't enough—packaging counts. Employers and executive consultants alike agree that a large percentage of able candidates don't make it beyond the initial screening process due to poorly constructed, poorly presented resumes. The underlying assumption is that if you can't communicate about yourself in a way that invites interest and attention, you aren't fully equipped to deal with today's highly communications-oriented work world. Like it or not, that's the way it is.

But of course *you* don't really need to worry, since, having reached this stage of your resume development, you can proceed to the final packaging with confidence and clarity.

The following packaging steps have been pre-tested and refined from several lifetimes of resume reading and writing by employment and counseling experts. We recommend that you follow them as exactly as you can. As you follow these final steps, remember what we said many pages back, that your resume not only *describes,* it also *demonstrates* your ability to handle basic written communication.

Typing and Typography

To prepare your resume for duplication, find the best professional typewriter you can within your area—an electric, heavy-duty business machine that is clean and in good operating order. Don't skimp on this. If you have to rent one (generally costs $35 to $50 per month) or pay someone to type your resume in order to get the best, don't hesitate to do so. With all that you have invested in the process to date, this is no place to start cutting back.

Follow these simple typing rules:

- Use a clear, dark typewriter ribbon (preferably cartridge).

- Make sure the name, address, and phone number are centered on the top.
- Use one-inch margins minimum on all sides.
- Don't make it look cramped—use plenty of white space.
- Highlight important titles by using caps and underlining.
- Use single space—double between paragraphs.

It is not advisable to have your entire resume professionally typeset by a printer or typesetter, as this is usually seen as graphic overkill and shows insecurity. It is all right to set type for major headings and name and address to highlight these areas. Most printers will be able to do this for you at a cost of $20 to $25. A less expensive way to do the headlining work yourself is to purchase from an art supply store a sheet or two of transfer type, which enables you to affix professional-looking headings to your original resume by simply rubbing the letters off the transfer sheet onto the desired location. You don't have to be a graphic designer to do this, but it helps to have a steady hand and good sense of organization. Bold headings can also be put in with typewriters that have changeable type elements. It's your own choice how much attention to pay to these areas. Review our samples (pages 154–194).

White Space

One thing you will notice about most good advertising layouts is the conscious use of empty space on the page, known in the ad trade as "air" or white space. It serves as a way of accenting what is on the page in a way that is restful on the eye and mind. It implies that you are confident enough in what you have to say that you don't need to fill every space. Create white space in your resume through wide margins, double spacing between major paragraphs, careful positioning of your name and address block, and use of indentions. Caution: Don't put in so much air that there isn't much else. Use our samples as guides for your own layout.

Layout

The purpose of the layout, or organization of your resume, is to attract the reader's eye to the most logical and powerful parts. To make it effortless for the reader to get the picture you wish to describe. A good layout is unobtrusive yet directs the eye unconsciously to the important parts. Some of the elements of your layout that you can work with are:

- UPPER CASE LETTERS—For headings or titles that are important. Use sparingly, as overuse tends to cancel out. Be consistent.
- Underlining—Can be used in the body of the resume to emphasize a dramatic result, accomplishment, or other highlight that you want the employer to see. Be careful that what you underline is, in fact, special, because if the reader doesn't agree, then the whole idea backfires. Also, use underlining sparingly, as it can cause the reader's attention to jump around and miss other parts.
- *Italics*—Not generally used, but if available on the typewriter it can be used in the same manner as underlining in the body of the resume.
- Highlighting—A very new and effective technique. Simply use a translucent color and highlighting pen to dramatize key accomplishments within the body of

the resume once it is printed. You can highlight different information for different employers. Best used at lower and middle range positions. A bit too artsy for top management.

• Indenting—Separates different types of information and makes the reader's job easier. Use two or (at most) three different levels as indicated by our samples.

• "Bullets"—These are points of punctuation (• or *) set in front of each item in a list of accomplishments or other results that are short separate points to be made.

First and Second Drafts

Don't expect to achieve the best layout styling and impact in your resume on the first draft. Plan to do two or three drafts—either by hand or typewriter. Once you have pulled the information together, edit ruthlessly, cutting back sentences that are too long, eliminating redundancies and confusing style.

Edit and Critique

Get the first or second draft critiqued by someone who is very good at grammar, spelling, and punctuation. Don't plan to do this yourself, as most of us have blind spots about our own errors. Please take this critique and editing function very seriously. A surprising percentage of resumes end up getting printed with errors that require redoing at a later date, or that cause embarrassment when you discover that you've been sending them out to potential employers.

In having your resume critiqued, make sure that the person doing the critiquing knows that you want him/her to be as tough as possible and not to make you feel good. Don't present it with the statement or question "Isn't this a good resume?" or "How do you like this?" Rather say, "Do you have any ideas how to make this stronger?" or "Please look for any errors." Thank that person for his/her input. Don't argue or explain. Just get it. You can decide later whether or not to take the advice. Give the editor a photocopy or carbon to work with.

The critique you want is essentially one that points out errors and lack of clarity. Avoid discussions of format, content, or emphasis unless the person critiquing is really an expert. There is a lot of outdated information floating around in the practices of some counselors and others who have been out of touch with employers' needs. There are also, unfortunately, many resume books that promote archaic and often erroneous information. In this book we have presented concepts and examples coming out of our extensive direct experience with job candidates who have been able to get interviews, and out of our involvement in the employment process with hundreds of personnel staff, supervisors, and managers. We may not have all the answers, but we are definitely operating at a pragmatic rather than theoretical level.

Below is a checklist of things to look for in critiquing your resume draft.

RESUME CRITIQUE CHECKLIST

_____ Material fits neatly on one page

_____ No spelling, grammar, or punctuation errors

_____ Typing is neat, clean, and professional looking

_____ Name, address, and telephone numbers are centered at top

_____ Margins at sides and bottom are at least one inch wide

_____ Layout makes reading easy

_____ No paragraphs are longer than ten to twelve lines

_____ Important titles are emphasized by underlining or capital letters where appropriate—and not overdone

_____ Indentions are used to organize information logically

_____ Action words are used to communicate accomplishments and results

_____ Extraneous and personal information (height, weight, age, sex, etc.) have been left out

_____ Sentences and paragraphs have been edited to eliminate unnecessary and redundant information

_____ Over-all appearance invites you to read it

_____ Resume demonstrates candidate's ability to produce results

Duplicating and Printing

At this point you should have a beautiful, edited, well-typed communication of your skills, abilities, and relevant work history—congratulations for that! You have virtually mastered the process. Time to go to press.

Do not send an original resume to an employer under any circumstances—it implies that you are a bit too eager for the job. Don't send a poor copy of it either.

Your resume should be printed by photo-offset process on a high quality paper stock by a local printer. In the photo-offset process, a printing plate is prepared right from your original, and the printed copies retain all (or give more) of the snap and crispness of the original. The cost for a hundred copies is around fifteen dollars or less—a small investment for a high class presentation. If you don't know a printer, please check in the yellow pages. Call two or three and get comparative quotes.

Have the printer use a good quality paper stock—not just the routine stuff. White stock is fine, and we feel that it is even better looking on an ivory, buff, or off-white quality paper—this tends to let the resume stand out against the virtual snowbank of other white letters, resumes, and the other paperwork that clutters most desks.

Why not run it off on your handy Xerox or photocopy machine? It just isn't good enough, that's why. The image frequently smears, the paper is usually fairly low grade, and the quality isn't consistent. At best, it gets a B—. We're pushing for straight A's.

And that—gentle and persevering readers—is The Perfect Resume. We did it—you and we. By the time you read this we've already done our celebrating and taken our cold shower to pull together the remaining pages in the book. Please treat yourself to a similar acknowledgment when your resume returns from the printer. Toast yourself with the knowledge that you are, in resume terms, better prepared than 95 percent of the job seekers in your ball park.

In Step 6 we'll show you how to put together a cover letter to go with your resume, and starting on pages 205–208 we'll provide some abbreviated job search techniques.

Step 6: The Perfect Cover Letter

Despite the perfection, clarity, and strong self-presentation of your resume, it is in fact a printed form—a fairly high level and conscious one, but a printed form nonetheless. It remains for the reader to interpret and project from the resume the things that he or she feels to be of value to that person's organization.

Sometimes this is done successfully, sometimes not; employment managers are just as fallible as anyone else. Obviously, with the well-thought-out resume just created, you have greatly improved your chances of getting the interviews you want. But now we want to remove as much of the remaining doubt as we possibly can from the employment equation.

The individual cover letters that accompany your resume when you mail them to employers can be as helpful to your job campaign as a personal introduction to your potential employer would be.

The purpose of the cover letter is to communicate to the employer a specific personalized message about your potential value to that organization. It generates interest in you from the person who counts. It is not difficult to write, and it adds a powerful element to your resume.

COVER LETTER RULES

RULE 1—ADDRESS IT TO A PARTICULAR PERSON BY NAME

Send your letter to the person who can make the hiring decision—by name. Personal letters get read far ahead of form letters. Think of your own experience when you open the mail—the letters addressed to you personally get read first. The form letters to "sir" or "madam" or "occupant" may not be read at all.

Call the firm with which you wish to interview, and find out the name (correct spelling, please) and title of the individual in charge of the department you would like to work in. Don't worry if it takes three or four calls. If you get stuck, call the president's office and find out from someone there who is in charge of the area you are interested in. Don't say that you are looking for a job. Say that you have some information to send and want to make sure it gets in the hands of the right person.

With a little practice you'll find there isn't much problem in retrieving the names and titles you want. After all, organizations need to maintain contact with their public. Don't make the mistake of aiming too high. Corporate presidents and board chairmen get lots of resumes because their names are so visible. Even with a good cover letter these are usually intercepted. Find a person at the department or division level—ideally, the person you would work for if you got the job.

RULE 2—COMMUNICATE SOMETHING PERSONAL

People who get a lot of mail are wary of form letters and have developed personal techniques to skim quickly before reading to see if, in fact, the letter has a message for them.

In your opening line, write something that is uniquely associated with the person, division, or organization and that will signal to the reader that you invested the time to communicate personally.

The likelihood of a personal response to your letter is directly related to the degree of personal attention you put into it in the first place. You get what you give.

Some typical "personal" opening lines are:

"I see that you have opened a new shopping mall on the western side of town."

"Dr. Foster in the economics department said that she had talked with you about your expansion plans."

"I understand that you have just received a new study grant from ACW."

Some basic research (see pages 205–206) is called for in preparing this opening.

RULE 3—ANSWER THE QUESTION "WHY SHOULD I SEE YOU?"

The work world operates on *value,* not need. You are of interest to a potential employer to the degree that they experience you as being valuable *to them,* not for what you are looking for *from them.*

In the body of your cover letter communicate some special way that your skills can be valuable to the potential employer. Create interest in yourself. This will require some basic understanding or research in your target field (pages 205–206 again), not a major research project, but mostly an expanded familiarity with the interests of the potential employer, and a willingness to show how you can make a contribution. Common sense helps as the following examples indicate:

"I feel that my organizational skills could help you in setting up your new customer service department. As you can see from my resume I have experience in handling service calls in a related field, and could help you train your people."

"My several years of work in the Old Salem restoration project could be valuable in your community museum. I believe I could also assist you in fund raising."

"I know that you are aware of the need for publicity and communication with your local community. My work in this area at school, plus my knowledge of the community, will assist you to get the exposure you want."

Don't be afraid to take a few risks in describing what you feel you could do for the employer. If you are not directly on target, even the fact that you are talking in terms of value rather than need will create interest.

Be careful not to set the letter in a negative tone and criticize or put down what the company has done. Communicate your ability to assist and support, not that you threaten what they do.

2301 Meadow Lane
Bull Shoals, Arkansas 72619
January 12, 1980

Dr. Frank Brown
Director of Chemistry
Seville University
Seville, Arkansas 72465

Dear Dr. Brown:

I read with interest your article in "New Science" about "Alternatives to Particulate Pollution." I have done intensive study into this subject and have come up with some theories which could be of value to you.

In addition to discovering a new technique for analyzing particulate content in minutes; I have several plans for a simple and inexpensive filter-type mechanism which can cut particulates up to 85%.

I have recently graduated with an M.S. in Chemistry from California Institute of Technology. My Master's thesis was "Analytical Methods in Air Pollution" to be published by University Press next fall.

I would like to meet you to further discuss the possibilities of our working together. I will call you in eight to ten days to set up an appointment.

Yours truly,

Jeanne MacGinnis
(801) 396-5555

RULE 4—USE THEIR LANGUAGE

Every field has its own jargon and technology. Use the right terms to indicate your ability and expertise. An excellent way to improve your knowledge of the nomenclature of the field is to read back issues of trade journals and articles by professionals in that particular field—see your librarian. Watch out for overkill.

29-24 Crescent Blvd.
Forest Hills NY 11433
October 12, 1979
(212) 666-4646

Mr. John Terriell
Accounting Manager
General Office Supply Co.
412 Norman Avenue
Wharfield NY 11352

Dear Mr. Terriell,

Jack Thatcher at the Chase Bank told me that General Office Supply
is opening a new branch in Forest Hills. I have dealt with your
company several times and am delighted to see that you will be
moving even closer to my home area.

As a member of the Forest Hills Communication Committee, I have
gained experience in all phases of bookkeeping as well as purchasing.
Your product lines are very familiar to me, as you have supplied
us with materials for our evening seminars and weekend meetings,
as well as our parties.

With my knowledge in these areas, I am sure that I could make a
contribution to your company in the new branch in Forest Hills.
I would like to meet with you to discuss some of these ideas
further. I will call you next week to arrange a meeting.

                              Yours truly,

                              Hilda Lebanon

                              Hilda Lebanon

RULE 5—ASK FOR THE INTERVIEW

Salespeople call this the "close"—the time when you ask for the business. In this case the "business" is a personal *meeting* (a more subtle word than interview). Ask for it. You can even suggest a date and time. Here are some closing statements:

"I am planning to take interviews at the end of school next month, and if possible would like to meet with you during the first week of May. I will call you to set up a possible date."

"I will be in your area on other business on the 13th of this month and would like to see you then if it's convenient."

452 South Rockline Avenue
Seneca, New York 11290
315-421-1890
January 23, 1979

Ms. Sandra Breuer
Curator of Impressionist Art
Museum of Modern Art
11 West 53rd Street
New York, NY 10020

Dear Ms. Breuer,

I recently read in "Art Forum" that the museum is planning a large Van Gogh exhibit next winter, with the cooperation of Amsterdam's two major museums. I was thrilled to hear that Americans will be able to see these masterpieces here for the first time ever.

I have recently graduated from Washington Square College at New York University. While attending, I was fortunate enough to spend one semester abroad. I became very involved with Amsterdam; the people and the sights, but mainly in the art. I spent many afternoons at the Rijksmuseum and others and I now possess an extensive knowledge of their collections.

I feel that my knowledge of Van Gogh's work, the city of Amsterdam and my general background in arts and letters could be of value to you in promoting this exhibit to young people. I would like to meet with you to discuss some ideas on the subject and I will call you in a week to ten days to set up a meeting.

Yours truly,

Ken Tyson

"Could we get together next week sometime to see if there is a mutual interest? I'll call your secretary to find out."

Notice that closing your cover letter this way makes it easy and natural for you to follow up with a phone call.

SPECIAL RESUME NOTES FOR COLLEGE STUDENTS

In the past few years we have visited over two hundred college campuses around the United States and Canada presenting our *Guerrilla Tactics in the Job Market* lecture series to students and career counselors. In these lectures and seminars, and individual meetings, we have had the opportunity to review and critique hundreds of graduating students' resumes as well as resume manuals used by career planning and placement offices.

As a counterpoint to this on-campus perspective, we have also had the opportunity to conduct interview training sessions with several thousand employers and recruiters, and as part of many of these training sessions to get feedback on their reactions to the resumes they receive from college students. The approximate verdict of the judges: 50 percent failing, 20 percent marginal to good, 20 percent good to very good, 10 percent excellent. The major complaints:

- Too much "factual" information (dates, titles, courses) and not enough presentation of accomplishments or results
- Takes too long to say too little
- Lack of strong self-presentation
- Poorly organized and laid out
- Poorly typed and printed
- Too much irrelevant information (age, weight, sex, health, etc.)

Much of the resume information available on college campuses is an outgrowth of an older school of resume preparation that saw the resume as an extension of, or substitute for, the job application—a purely factual profile. It also reflects an unfortunately more basic attitude: that new graduates have little of practical value to offer the work world and shouldn't be too "boastful." We don't buy this assumption, nor do a growing majority of modern career counseling and placement professionals. New college graduates have an enormous amount to contribute to the work world—well beyond their grade point averages and major studies. The college experience has many parallels to the work world experience. Students should be willing to acknowledge and communicate their campus achievements and accomplishments. Studies have shown that employers look well beyond grades and courses studied in determining who to hire. Here are some points and reminders for college students:

- Consider using the functional format, since there isn't much job chronology to report.
- Include human factors that go beyond courses studied: organizational ability, leadership, budgeting, willingness to take on a variety of assignments, etc.
- Talk about the things you accomplished in non-classroom activities: clubs, fraternities, committees, school events.
- Beg, borrow, or rent a top-notch professional typewriter that will make your resume snap with authority.
- Be willing to spend a little to have your resume printed. Don't succomb to the convenient photocopier.
- Have your draft triple checked for typos, and errors in grammar and punctuation.
- Never go beyond one page.
- Be proud of your accomplishments— and show it.

See the following four sample resumes:

Booking Agent

JAMES AGEE
291 RUSSELL AVENUE
BRIDGEPORT, CONNECTICUT 06606
203-733-0859

Targeted

EDUCATION: B.A. University of Bridgeport   1980

JOB TARGET: Booking Agent

CAPABILITIES:

* Create, develop and manage jazz and rock groups.
* Develop and implement well-planned budgets and schedules for bands.
* Scout talent for purpose of creating new groups.
* Establish and direct showcase presentations to expose new talent to the public.
* Negotiate fees.
* Write press releases and album covers.

ACCOMPLISHMENTS:

* Promoted five concerts in 2000 seat auditorium for college audiences.
* Created and managed two progressive jazz groups that traveled nine states in 60 days.
* Supervised spring concert series featuring new talent and attended by over 1200 students.
* Wrote numerous reviews on new album releases for college newspapers.
* Booked jazz bands on several campuses and in local clubs.

WORK HISTORY:

1979-80   Chairman - Concert Committee
            University of Bridgeport

1978-79   Music Critic - The Student Chronicle
            U.B. College newspaper

1976-78   Manager/Agent - The Brothers Three and the
            Music Students

Research Assistant

DANIEL M. KARLOFF
309 BERKELEY DRIVE
SYRACUSE, N.Y. 13210
(315) 492-8711

Targeted

COLLEGE STUDENT

EDUCATION: B.A. Syracuse University   1980   Urban Studies

JOB TARGET: RESEARCH ASSISTANT WITH AN URBAN AND REGIONAL PLANNING FIRM

CAPABILITIES:

- Write complete and detailed research reports.
- Edit written materials for content and grammar.
- Work long hours without physical stress or annoyance.
- Communicate effectively with librarians and others required to support research work.
- Read and take useful notes on detailed or dense materials.
- Type reports, memos, and letters in draft form.
- Receive and carry out complicated instructions and tasks.
- Sketch and draw charts and other visual materials required to supplement explanatory text.

ACHIEVEMENTS:

- Edited college political magazine and wrote articles on social issues.
- Successfully researched background material for textbook on urban economics written by Professor Alfred Hinderman.
- Won Senior Prize for essay on crime in urban ghettos.
- Ran successful dormitory newspaper business.
- Maintained A- average throughout college career.

WORK HISTORY:

1977 - Present   Syracuse University Dormitory Council
                      - Newspaper Business Manager
                      - Newspaper Deliverer

1979 - Present   Professor Alfred Hinderman
                      - Research Assistant

1977 - 1978   Syracuse Democratic Committee
                      - Campaign Worker

1976 - 1979   Karloff Construction
                      - Laborer

Sports Writer

BOB SAMPSON
11 RANDALL AVENUE
MADISON, WISCONSIN 53715
(608) 433-2981

Functional

EDUCATION:

1980   B.A. Journalism, University of Wisconsin

WRITING:

- Wrote articles for the sports section of college newspaper.

- Had three articles published in city newspaper.

- Served as assistant editor of the sports section of college newspaper.

- Wrote sports editorials for the final edition of the Badger News - school newspaper.

SPORTS:

- Played four years college basketball.

- Nominated 'Player of the Year' in state college basketball.

- Coached high school basketball players at summer clinic.

- Responsible for three high school players going on to college with scholarships.

COMMUNICATION/RADIO/VIDEO:

- Announced live broadcasts of football games on college radio.

- Wrote and delivered nightly sports news for radio on football weekends.

- Assisted in developing basketball training via video.

- Delivered sports promotional spots on local college radio station.

WORK HISTORY:

1978-1980	BADGER NEWS, University of Wisconsin - Madison	Assistant Editor
		Sports Writer
1977-1978	BADGER RADIO, University of Wisconsin - Madison	Radio Sports Announcer
1976-1980 Summers	CAYUGA BASKETBALL CLINIC, Green Bay, Wisconsin	Coach and Instructor

Editor/Writer

KARLA SALVEN
333 DREXAL DRIVE
PITMAN, NEW JERSEY   08225
(609) 432-0488

Functional

COLLEGE STUDENT

EDUCATION:

1980   B.A. Journalism/Communications, Glassboro State College
                                        Glassboro, New Jersey

WRITING:

* Wrote full page essays on controversial and political issues for college yearbook.
* Researched and wrote birth announcements for daily county-wide paper.
* Reported on local political meetings for daily local paper.
* Reported on pertinent college issues for college newspaper.

EDITING:

* Edited newspaper articles on local events.
* Assisted in making all editorial decisions for college yearbook which won second place in national competition.
* Selected and edited all copy for yearbook.
* Insured accuracy of all information for college freshman general information guide.

MANAGING:

* Selected and hired photographers, and managed the scheduling of all senior class photo sessions.
* Coordinated photographic shootings between five photographers with 143 groups and 203 events.
* Oversaw and approved design and layout of yearbook for two years.
* Coordinated and designed freshman orientation handbook.

PHOTOGRAPHY:

* Shot pictures of local events and groups for daily paper.
* Shot and selected photos for a variety of college publications.

EXPERIENCE:

1979 - 1980   SHADOW - Freshman Orientation Handbook   Editor
                 Glassboro State College

1978 - 1980   Mainland Times, Vineland, N.J.   Writer/Editor - Local Events
(part-time)

1977 - 1980   IMAGE, College Yearbook   Assistant Editor
                 Glassboro State College

1977 - 1978   BORO NEWS, Glassboro, N.J.   Writer - Announcements
(part-time)

SPECIAL NOTES FOR WOMEN REENTERING THE JOB MARKET

The first major job-finding programs we ran were in the late 1960s, and were for women who were entering or reentering the work world after an absence of several years while rearing a family. Since then, what started as a trickle from the kitchen faucet has expanded to a social torrent. The movement of women into the work force has become the major growth area of our labor force.

Even more importantly, much of this growth has been into non-traditional work roles. Legal and social forces combine to provide a new imperative to open the best jobs to all sexes and races *if they can get the job done*—an important part of the small print.

The natural tendency for many women who have been out of the work world for years is to downplay what they have done in paid employment. Like college students, they tend to devalue their homelife experiences, and are unwilling to demonstrate the potential relevance to the world of paid work.

All experience counts. Much of what you have done at home or school will be applicable to your worklife ambitions. And, of course, much won't. Your task in the resume preparation is to actively identify the parts of your life that demonstrate your ability, *and willingness,* to make a contribution. Some pointers:

- Pay particular attention to the Career Discovery Process in the beginning of this book—do the exercises.
- Experiment with the functional format and the resume alternative.
- Emphasize the human factors in your career inventory: organizational skills, ability to communicate, supervisory ability, people skills.
- Familiarize yourself with topics in the work world—read trade journals, business publications, books. Get exposure to actual working environments—through temporary service work, volunteering and working with friends and relatives who are in business.
- Make a list of twenty friends, professional contacts, ex-professors, neighbors, and relatives who could help you develop additional leads for your resume.
- Stretch yourself—further than you may have thought possible—get rid of any tendencies for self-disparagement or playing small. In addition to your resume demonstrate your abilities in the way you dress, the quality of your communication, your ability to discover opportunities to create value for others.
- Get support in the form of positive reinforcement and honest critique from family and friends. Use all available resources.

See the following four sample resumes:

WOMEN REENTERING   ELLEN SIMPSON   Functional
                    203 WARREN AVENUE
                  SPRING LAKE, N.J. 07762
                     (201) 449-6793

TEACHING:

- Instructed large community groups on issues related to child abuse.

- Taught interested volunteers how to set-up community child abuse programs.

- Ran workshops for parents of abused children.

- Instructed public school teachers on signs and symptoms of potential child abuse.

COUNSELING:

- Consulted with parents for probable child abuse and suggested courses of action.

- Worked with social workers on individual cases, both in urban and suburban settings.

- Counseled single parents on appropriate coping behaviors.

- Handled pre-intake interviewing of many individual abused children.

ORGANIZATION/COORDINATION:

- Coordinated transition of children between original home and foster home.

- Served as liaison and child abuse educator between community health agencies and schools.

- Wrote proposal to state for county funds to educate single parents and teachers.

VOLUNTEER WORK HISTORY:

1974 - 1980   COMMUNITY MENTAL HEALTH CENTER, Freehold, N.J.
                Volunteer Coordinator - Child Abuse Program

1970 - 1974   C.A.R.E. - Child-Abuse Rescue-Education,
                Albany Park, N.J.
                County Representative

EDUCATION:

1960   B.S. Sociology DOUGLASS COLLEGE, New Brunswick, N.J.

Sales/Fund-raising

ALICIA ARNOLD
242 NORTH END DRIVE
BETHEL, KENTUCKY 05394
(217) 643-0972

Functional

SALES/FUNDRAISING:

* Sold Avon products to over 500 private clients, grossing $10,000 in sales in one year.
* Raised over $300,000 for the American Heart Association through a Bike-a-thon.
* Increased Saturday sales in women's clothing boutique by 30% in six months.

MANAGING:

* Managed small boutique in owner/manager's absence.
* Planned and coordinated all details in producing Bike-a-thon.
* Oversaw promotional activities for Bike-a-thon.
* Managed all planning and administration for Cub Scout outings.

SUPERVISING:

* Supervised a staff of five volunteers for the American Heart Association.
* Supervised all activities of ten Cub Scouts for two years.
* Managed group of 75 Cub Scouts and seven volunteer adults on weekend district-wide camping trip.

EXPERIENCE:

1978 - 1980   ANNIE PINK'S BOUTIQUE
                  Saleswoman - Part-time

1972 - 1980   AVON
                  Sales Representative

1975 - 1976   AMERICAN HEART ASSOCIATION
                  Manager of Bike-a-thon

1969 - 1971   BOY SCOUTS OF AMERICA
                  Den Mother - Troop 405

EDUCATION:

1978   Courses in Business Management Bethel Community College
                                                  Bethel, Kentucky

Editor

WOMEN REENTERING

MARIANNE FURMAN
656 WYNDHAM ROAD
TEANECK, N.J. 07666
(201) 682-1342

Functional

EDITING

Responsible for production editing of social science textbooks for major publisher. Managed complete book production process from copy editing to printing and distribution. Successfully produced over a dozen textbooks.

WRITING

Wrote major best-selling study guides for fiction including Anna Karenina, War and Peace, Don Quixote, and four plays by Ibsen. Wrote introduction and recipes for widely-read community cookbook.

RESEARCH

Studied, wrote, published and widely distributed study materials about the lives and works of Tolstoy, Cervantes, and Ibsen. Developed and shared research techniques that cut participants' study time by 25%.

THERAPY

Counseled as psychotherapist dozens of individuals, couples, families and groups in mental health centers. Established successful experimental methods based on Viola Spolin's theatre games.

EDUCATION

M.S. Fairleigh Dickinson University - 1977
Clinical Psychology

Program Developer
WOMEN RE-ENTERING

BEVERLY RHODES
200 AVENEL WAY
WASHINGTON, D.C. 20034
202-791-1774

Functional

WORK EXPERIENCE:

TRAINING:
Wrote training manual for the care of isolated patients in nursing homes. Developed remedial training concepts for community volunteers - working with disadvantaged youth. Created awareness training program for airline industry personnel to foster better understanding of handicapped passenger needs. Wrote proposal for the training of counselors working with ex-offenders, resulting in a $250m Federal funding.

TESTING:
Administered tests to ex-offenders and high school students using various skills tests, including the Wexler and MMPI. Evaluated, tested and developed psychological and skill profiles. Consulted with psychologist on test results and client direction. Referred clients to various self-help organizations as a result of testing.

ORGANIZING:
Organized crafts, games and field trips for neighborhood youth during summer vacation. Counseled 50 teenage women in birth control methods and prenatal care. Delivered lectures to various community organizations on the need to support mental health programs.

WORK HISTORY:

1975 - Present
Volunteer with numerous community and mental health organizations.

1974 - 75
National Airlines
Consultant in Awareness Training for Handicapped Passengers

EDUCATION:

1973
M.S.   George Washington University   Social Services

SAMPLE RESUMES

On the following pages are samples of resumes selected from our files as representing the principles set out in this book. We consider them to be examples of the highest form of the resume writing art. We have included a variety of occupations as well as types and styles of resumes and levels of experience. Names and addresses have, of course, been changed.

The sample resumes are arranged according to career fields. You will also find a Resume Selector which gives the resume format as a cross-reference. Identify a field and locate the page alphabetically to review that resume.

If your job target field is not directly represented, don't worry, for many of the resumes in other fields will be of value as a guide. After you have selected the format of your resume, review a number of examples in the same format.

Following the illustrated resumes, we have given a number of examples of job fields not represented by resumes of their own. Much of the basic information in these related paragraphs comes to us courtesy of the *Dictionary of Occupational Titles.**

The first three resumes are before-and-after examples. Try this: before you look at the "after," see how you would critique the "before," indicating the changes you would make.

---

* U.S. Department of Labor, Fourth Edition. Washington, D.C. 1977.

Index to Sample Resumes

Job Target Field	Sample Paragraph	Chronological	Functional	Targeted	Resume Alternative	Special Interest For College Students	Special Interest For Women Re-entering Job Market
Account Executive	195						
Accountant — Recent College Graduate				160		160	
Accounts Payable/ Receivable Clerk	195						
Activities Planner — College	195					195	
Administrative Assistant	195						
Administrative Coordinator					123		
Advertising Clerk	196						
Advertising Media Planner		161					
Art Director	196						
Artist			162				
Assistant Plant Manager (before)		154					
Assistant Plant Manager (after)			155				
Assistant TV Producer (before)			158				
Assistant TV Producer (after)			159				
Auditor	196						
Banker		164					
Booking Agent				139		139	
Buyer, Fashion			165				
Certified Public Accountant	196						

Job Target Field	Sample Paragraph	Chronological	Functional	Targeted	Resume Alternative	Special Interest For College Students	Special Interest For Women Re-entering Job Market
Chemist/Manager			166				
Clerk — Civil Service	197						
Communications Consultant	197						
Community Developer	197						
Coordinator — Engineering			17				
Copywriter			167				
Counseling Director	197						
Counselor/ Coordinator			144				144
Date Processing — College Graduate			168				
Dental Assistant	198						
Design Engineer		171	95				
Die Designer		170					
Drafter	198						
Editor			146				146
Editorial Assistant	198						
Educational Therapist	198						
Electrical Engineer				169			
Employee Benefits Executive				62			
Employment Counselor		87					

Job Target Field	Sample Paragraph	Chronological	Functional	Targeted	Resume Alternative	Special Interest For College Students	Special Interest For Women Re-entering Job Market
Executive Secretary				172			
Fashion Coordinator	199						
Fund Raiser	199						
Guidance Director	199						
Health Services — College	199						
Hospital Administrator				173			
Industrial Hygienist	199						
Journalist			142			142	
Lawyer			174				
Librarian			175				
Lobbyist	199						
Mailroom Supervisor	200						
Management Consultant	200						
Management Trainee	200						
Manager, Business			176				
Manager — Chemicals Procurement (before)		156					
Manager — Chemicals Procurement (after)		157					
Manager/Executive		177					
Manager/Insurance			178				

Job Target Field	Sample Paragraph	Chronological	Functional	Targeted	Resume Alternative	Special Interest For College Students	Special Interest For Women Re-entering Job Market
Manager, Retail Store	200						
Manager/Technical				179			
Market Analyst/ Researcher		180					
Marketing Manager				181			
Mechanical Engineer	201						
Medical Record Administrator	201						
Merchandise Manager	201						
Nutritionist			182				
Package Designer	201						
Personnel Supervisor			183				
Photographer			184				
Plant Engineer	202						
Program Developer		185					
Project Director	202						
Public Relations			186				
Public Relations Representative	202						
Rehabilitative Physiotherapist				187			
Research Nutritionist	202						
Researcher				140		140	

Job Target Field	Sample Paragraph	Chronological	Functional	Targeted	Resume Alternative	Special Interest For College Students	Special Interest For Women Re-entering Job Market
Residence Counselor	203						
Retail Management		188					
Sales, Auto			163				
Sales/Fundraising			145				145
Sales Manager	203						
Sales/Retail			189				
Secretary		190					
Securities Analyst		191					
Senior Credit Analyst				105			
Social Service Administrator			147				147
Social Worker		192					
Sociologist	203						
Student Affairs Director	203						
Systems Analyst	204						
Tabulating Machine Operator	204						
Teacher				193			
Teacher's Aide	204						
Travel Agent		194					
Writer — Sports			141			141	

Assistant Plant Manager

BEFORE

TOM KANDOWSKI
497 Christy St.
Carteret, New Jersey 07008   Telephone 201 546-3876

PERSONAL	Married 6 ft. 190 lb. 27 years old

EDUCATION   Attended Middlesex County College for two years, Majoring in Liberal Arts-Business Administration.

Attended Trenton State College, majoring in Political Science. Received Bachelor of Arts degree in December, 1972, with a 3.52 cumulative average.

Studied Stationary Engineering at Middlesex County Vocational School at night in 1974-75. Received a Blue Seal engineer's license in August, 1975.

Studied Basic Machine Shop at Middlesex County Vocational School at night in 1975-76.

SCHOLASTIC ACHIEVEMENTS   Graduated with Honors from Trenton State College. Was on the Dean's List for four semesters. Was one of the representatives of the Political Science Dept. to the National Model United Nations Conference held in New York in 1972.

WORK EXPERIENCE   6/66-10/69 Produce and Frozen Foods clerk at Anderson's Foodtown, 989 Port Reading Ave., Port Reading, N.J., part-time while in school, and full-time during summers.

6/70-10/70 Canning Machine Operator at Greater Northeastern Tank Corp. (GNTC), Lafayette St., Carteret, N.J.

4/73-7/76 Oiler at Northern Railroad, Port Reading, N.J., for two years. Then promoted to Maintenance Machinist in charge of mechanical work. Duties also included pipefitting and operating steam boilers, engines, lathes, and other machine shop equipment.

Worked part-time for several years with a licensed electrical contractor (Lewis Electric Co.), installing residential and industrial services, equipment and wiring.

11/76-Present Maintenance Technician at Technicians, Inc. (Data Processing Center), 3678 Park Ave., Metuchen, N.J. Duties included Climate Control and Building Maintenance.

BACKGROUND   Brought up in Carteret area and attended local schools. Delivered Newark Star Ledger newspapers for five years. Member of Carteret High School wrestling team for two years. Member of the Cub Scouts and Boy Scouts for several years.

INTERESTS   I enjoy reading, fresh-water fishing, camping, music, sports, and traveling.

Assistant Plant Manager   Functional

AFTER
                           Tom Kandowski
                           497 Christy St.
                           Carteret, N.J. 07008
                           201-546-3876

                           WORK EXPERIENCE

ADMINISTRATIVE: Coordinated plant service activities, including
                           installation, maintenance, and repair of equipment
                           for a 30,672 ft. data processing center. Developed
                           preventive maintenance schedules and handled all
                           follow through.

MECHANICAL: Responsible for repairing and maintaining all mech-
                           anical aspects of a railroad coal-dumper, including
                           bearing replacements, pump overhauls, and general
                           machine repairs.

PIPEFITTING: Made extensive steam line alterations and additions
                           following a conversion from coal to #6 oil firing
                           of three boilers totaling 1250 horsepower. Was also
                           involved in replacing sections of 12-inch boiler headers.

ELECTRICAL: Assisted a licensed electrical contractor in installing
                           residential and industrial services, equipment, and wiring

STATIONARY
ENGINEERING: Operated and maintained four piston valve steam
                           engines; maintained four slide valve steam engines,
                           and two duplex feedwater pumps. Also kept watch on
                           two firetube and one watertube boilers generating
                           150 psi steam. Was responsible for preparing this
                           equipment for insurance inspections.

                           WORK HISTORY

1976-Present   Technicians, Inc.
                           Maintenance Technician.

1973-1976   Northern Railroad- Coal-dumping Facility. Started
                           as an Oiler, then promoted to Maintenance Machinist.

1971-1973   Lewis Electric Company. Electrician's Assistant.

EDUCATION: B.S. Degree, Trenton State College. With honors.

                           Stationary Engineering, Middlesex County Vocational
                           School. Blue-Seal license.

Manager Chemicals Procurement   Chronological

BEFORE

JOHN HAVLOWE
82 Sherwood Street
Wildwood, New Jersey   07886
(201) 336-9834

BIRTHDATE:	January 18, 1931
HEALTH:	Excellent
HEIGHT:	5' 11"
WEIGHT:	185 lbs.
MARITAL STATUS:	Married, two dependent children

OBJECTIVE: To obtain the position of Purchasing Manager or Director
with a company that promotes individual initiative and
allows for individual application of Management expertise.

EDUCATION: Upsala College, East Orange, New Jersey
Chemistry and Business

Also 280 hours of various management courses sponsored
by Chemicals & Pharmaceuticals, Ltd., and Allied Metals
& Alloys Company

EMPLOYMENT:

1975 - Present: Allied Metals & Alloys Company

Corporate Manager - Chemicals Procurement

Responsible for managing a corporate Procurement group
which purchases the major chemical raw materials for
over 100 consuming plants in the U.S. Commodity
responsibility includes pulp and paper chemicals, plastic
resins, inks, waxes, coatings, solvents, plastic film and
sheet, and lignosulfonates.

1974 - 1975:   Allied Metals & Alloys Company

Materials Manager

Designed and implemented necessary systems and procedures
to establish purchasing function for M & T Chemicals, a
subsidiary of Allied Metals & Alloys. Implemented a cost
reduction program resulting in significant savings to
the corporation. Coordinated purchasing activities
between Corporate Purchasing and M & T Chemicals.

1969 - 1973:   Chemicals & Pharmaceuticals, Ltd.

Purchasing Agent

Was responsible for negotiating for approximately
$40 million of specialty and commodity raw materials.
Contributed significantly to Allied's cost reduction
program. Performed liaison function between Corporate
Purchasing and Allied of Canada, Ltd. Implemented
program to improve reporting systems between plants
and Purchasing.

Manager Chemicals Procurement Chronological

AFTER

JOHN HAVLOWE
82 Sherwood Street
Wildwood, New Jersey 07886
201-336-9834

WORK EXPERIENCE:

1975-
Present   <u>Allied Metals & Alloys Company</u>, MANAGER CHEMICALS PROCUREMENT

Manage a corporate procurement group which purchases the major chemical raw materials for over 100 consuming plants in the U. S. Commodity responsibility includes pulp and paper chemicals, plastic resins, inks, waxes, coatings, solvents plastic film and sheet, and lignosulfonates. Direct six professional buyers and non-exempt employees. Designed, developed and implemented cost reduction programs saving over $1MM per year. Initiated program in support of Hazardous Waste Disposal project. Participated in strategy planning and negotiations for key raw materials.

1974-1975   <u>Allied Metals & Alloys Company</u>, MATERIALS MANAGER

Designed and implemented necessary systems and procedures to establish purchasing function for M&T Chemicals, subsidiary of ACC. Coordinated purchasing activities between Corporate Purchasing and M&T.

1969-1974   <u>Chemicals & Pharmaceuticals, Ltd.</u>, PURCHASING AGENT

Negotiated for approximately $40MM of specialty and commodity raw materials. Contributed significantly to Allied's cost reduction program. Performed liaison function between Corporate Purchasing and Allied of Canada, Ltd. Implemented program to improve reporting systems between plants and Purchasing.

1964-1969   <u>Thioking Chemical Corporation</u>, TECHNICAL SPECIALIST II

Performed research, development and scale-up on advanced aerospace polymers. Invented seven materials for which patents were awarded.

EDUCATION:

Upsala College, New Jersey
Chemistry and Business

Various management courses sponsored by Allied Metals & Alloys Company and Chemicals & Pharmaceuticals, Ltd.

Assistant TV Producer   Functional

**COLLEGE GRADUATE
NO PAID WORK EXPERIENCE
BEFORE**

RESUME
MARIAN WILSON

Career Goal: Entry level position in TV Production

Home Address: 225 Maitland Ave.
                 Teaneck, New Jersey 07666
                 (201) 686-1210

Local Address: 5 Orkney Rd. #4
                 Brighton, Mass. 02146
                 (617) 237-2068

Born: March 2, 1955
                 Copaigue, New York

Education: 1973-1974: Elementary Education major at
                 the School of Education, Northeastern University
                 1974-1976: Senior at the School of Public
                 Communications, Northeastern University.
                         Major: Broadcasting and Film
                         Minor: Sociology

                 High School: 1973 graduate of Teaneck High

1976:   Work at T·V. Graphics, distributing equipment,
                 at Northeastern University's School of
                 Communications.

1976:   Audio Crew for Northeastern University
                 Alumni film.

1975:   School T.V. production presented at public showing.

1974:   Volunteer work for Northeastern University's
                 closed-circuit radio station, WTBU. Research
                 and on air.

Special Skills:

     Experienced in video equipment including porta-paks,
     studio cameras, mixing and switching boards and slide
     machine. Experience with Audio console including cart
     machine, revox and 350 tape machines. Experienced in
     Super 8mm cameras, viewers, and splicers.

References:

     Will be furnished upon request.

Assistant TV Producer

AFTER

Functional
No Dates

MARIAN WILSON
225 Maitland Ave. Teaneck, N.J. 07666
201-686-1210

TELEVISION

Produced and directed the following video productions: The Art of Batiking, The Impossible Dream, The Creative Process, and Wildlife Conservation. Organized all aspects: scriptwriting, audio selection and placement, set design--including furniture building and prop acquisition, lighting design and crew, casting, making slides and cue cards; planning camera shots, angles and composition.

FILM

Produced and directed the following: Everybody is a Star and Love is a Beautiful Thing. Handled camera work, editing, splicing, lighting and soundtrack. Designed and produced all graphics.

RADIO

Produced a tape demonstrating special effects including echo, reverberations, and speed distortion. Developed a 20 minute documentary: handled interviewing, narration, editing and splicing, and final taping.

TECHNICAL SKILLS

Operate:
for T.V.--studio cameras, porta-paks, and switching panel;
for film--various super 8mm cameras, viewers, splicers, and 16mm projectors;
for radio--audio console, turntables, various tape machines, handle cueing and mixing.

EDUCATION

B.S. Broadcasting and Film Northeastern University, 1977
Third Class Operator Permit F.C.C., 1976

Recent College Graduate
Accountant

Targeted

JOANNE A. RABAK
820 Westerfield Avenue
Minneapolis, Minnesota 55042
(612) 595-8283

ACCOUNTING DEPARTMENT MANAGER

CAPABILITIES:

.Manage large groups of people with ease
.Analyze vast amounts of data into relevant financial
 statistics
.Perform detailed customer audits
.Train clerical workers to handle large accounting functions
.Create strategies to improve secure company financial base
.Develop systems and procedures for all phases of accounting
.Produce clearly understandable financial statements;
 monthly and yearly

ACCOMPLISHMENTS:

.Conducted extensive audits of clients.
.Devised specific tests for auditing use.
.Created special programs for financial analysis in small
 non-profit firms.
.Supervised daily operation of large accounting department.
.Wrote and researched a detailed study of marketing.
.Administered all trustee-related aspects of bankruptcy
 proceedings.
.Handled credit analyses and references and made credit
 recommendations.

WORK EXPERIENCE:

1976-Present   Karpster and Halbrand, Inc.   Staff B Accountant

1971-74   Barnard College   Administrative Assistant

1968-71   Osterberg, Shindler, Harmon & Rostner, P.C.
                                                 Paraprofessional in Bankruptcy

EDUCATION:

1978   University of Minnesota Graduate School of Business
                MBA - Accounting

1968   Barnard College
                B.A. - History

Advertising Media Planner   Chronological

SANDY HARTFORD

425 West 68th Street
New York, New York 10018
(212) 877-0574

1975-Present   DOBBS, DANE, & KRONBACH, INC.   New York City

Media Planner. Analyze marketing objectives, formulate media strategies and recommend best media plans
for national package goods accounts. Communicate
media plans in writing and direct client presentations.
Responsible for $6.0 million multi-media account with
heavy television as well as $4.0 million heavy print
media account. Supervise one assistant planner.

Assistant Media Planner. Tabulated budget, quarterly
reports and spot television recaps. Operated time-
sharing computer system. Contributed to all media
planning activities such as extensive individual
market research on television usage. Participated
in strenuous media department training program.

1974-1975   KOHENY, SHALLER, MAYWOOD & GILBERT, INC. New York City

Media Buyer. Formulated media plans for all direct
marketing clients of the agency. Accounts included
Fargo's Department Store credit cards. Placed advertisements in major publications and monitored responses.

1972-1974   STIX, SCRUGGS & BARNEY, INC.   Chicago, Illinois

Media Buyer. Negotiated broadcast rates for direct
marketing clients. Assisted in traffic, light production of print, casting and production of radio and
T.V. commercials.

EDUCATION:

1972   B.S.   Bradley University

Artist   Functional

h(212)843-8990/w(212)345-7880

PASTE-UP/MECHANICALS   Produced paste-ups and mechanicals for the
GRAPHIC DESIGN   weekly "close" of Newsday magazine.

                              Designed brochures, booklists, selected type,
                              conceptualized and produced monthly silkscreen
                              posters, and planned displays for a major metro-
                              politan library.

TECHNICAL ILLUSTRATION   Mastered "LeRoy" lettering technique and created
JUNIOR ARTIST/FORMS DESIGNER technical illustrations for research publication
                              in the department of Photo-optics at the State
                              University of New York at Buffalo.

                              Designed and executed business and academic forms,
                              charts, graphs, brochures. Designed (with calligra-
                              phy) certificates and awards in the department of
                              Management Systems of the State University of
                              New York at Buffalo.

DRAWING BOARD ARTIST   Interfaced between client and printer from the
FREE-LANCE ARTIST/PHOTOGRAPHER drawing board in a commercial printing shop.
                              Produced numerous printed materials from business
                              cards to annual reports; supervised typesetter.

                              Supervised a commercial photographic studio and
                              undertook diverse free-lance jobs including pro-
                              ducing a 3 x 5 foot map of the State University
                              campus, large lettering assignments, portrait and
                              product photography for private individuals, and
                              slide shows for a hospital and the University.

Free-Lance Artist: 1977-Present
State University of New York, Buffalo, New York: 1974-1977
Len Koch, Inc. (commercial printing) Smithtown, New York: 1976
Buffalo Public Library, Buffalo, New York: 1972-1974
Newsday, Inc., Chicago, Illinois: 1971-1972

B.A. - General Studies/Social Sciences: the University of Chicago. 1971.
One year of commercial and fine arts courses: the School of Visual Arts. 1974.

Ms. Strong is an artist. She can use strong graphics—she's in that field. She used a combination format since her work history is free-lance and she's had a lot of jobs. Her job target is graphic design.

Sales, Auto   Functional

WARREN A. JAMES
517 HEART AVENUE
SEATTLE, WASHINGTON 98112

(206) 348-0529

AUTOMOBILE SALES/SERVICE:

Sold personal cars for profit after extensive use. Purchased
numerous used cars at low cost and sold them all for profit.
Handled more than 200 cars over the past 40 years. Employed as
a mechanic in early career. Supervised the maintenance and
repair of 48 vehicles while in the Armed Services. During that
time, was in charge of truck parts replacement for 215 Army vehicles
of the Battalion.

TECHNICAL SERVICES:

Coordinated customer accounts for packing of coffee, nuts and
bakery products. Furnished packing information and style containers necessary for their individual products and packing procedures. Had knowledge of customer packing procedures and was
able to reduce material costs for the company. Cost savings were
in excess of 25% per annum.

LABORATORY TECHNICAL SERVICE:

Set up test packs using less costly materials to determine shelf
life. Supervised group to conduct actual testing procedures.
Reduced tin coating on cans when tin became expensive and in
short supply through experimentation and follow-up.

WORK HISTORY:

ALLIED METAL CORPORATION........................1957 to present

    Technical Service Representative..........1969 to present

    Laboratory Technician....................1957 to 1969

AUTOMOBILE SALES/SERVICE (avocation)...........1957 to present

Total career change. He emphasizes skills practiced at his hobby.

Banker

MAHANI L. KATASHEMI

4060 Boulevard East Apt. 145
West New York, New Jersey 07190
Home: 201-863-8542
Office: 212-792-5360

Chronological

WORK EXPERIENCE:

FEDERAL RESERVE BANK OF NEW YORK   1975-Present

Operations Analyst: Responsible for developing proposals to top
management for operational reviews, organizing and managing the task
forces to conduct the reviews, documenting and presenting recommendations to top management, and coordinating this Bank's efforts with
similar initiatives in the Federal Reserve System. Major accomplishments include:

* Initiated, organized and managed a review of bank
  examinations and bank applications processing
  activities. Annual savings - $500,000.

* Developed multi-year plan, capital and operating
  budgets for the 185 person Foreign Department and
  analyzed costs of foreign exchange and investment
  transactions.

UNITED NATIONS DEVELOPMENT PROGRAM   1973-1975

Planning Officer: Responsible for program planning, resource allocation and evaluation of a $100 million program of technical and
capital assistance to developing countries in the area of population
control and economic development. Major accomplishments include:

* Organized and supervised a ten-month, 15 person
  study of the world contraceptive market, sponsored
  jointly by UNDP and the Ford Foundation.

* Developed a model-based forecasting system for program
  planning, management and control.

* Developed population control projects for countries in
  East Africa and the Middle East.

EDUCATION:

NEW YORK UNIVERSITY, GRADUATE SCHOOL OF BUSINESS   Ph.D.   1978
MASSACHUSETTS INSTITUTE OF TECHNOLOGY   M.S. in Management 1973
HARVEY MUDD COLLEGE   B.S. in Systems
                                                    Engineering & Physics
                                                    1969

Buyer, Fashion   MARYANN CORDELLO   Functional
1358 Wacker Drive
Chicago, Illinois
(312) 765-2190

PURCHASING/RETAIL AND CATALOG

- Selected merchandise for retail
- Determined price strategy and mark-up
- Examined merchandise and selected colors
- Prepared contracts

PRODUCT DEVELOPMENT

- Initiated changes in products to increase sales
- Analyzed merchandise for defects in design and material to improve quality of merchandise
- Analyzed comparative merchandise

ADMINISTRATOR

- Coordination, implementation and supervision of all office records
- Acted as liaison between sources and retail stores
- Coordinated purchase orders and responded to service of supply questions
- Trained employees from the Buyer's Assistant Training Program

WORK HISTORY   1968 - Present

Shore Radnor & Co.
Fashion Buying Office - New York

- Buyer's Assistant   1975 - Present
- Clerical Assistant Senior   1968 - 1975

EDUCATION/TRAINING

Fluent in Italian
Morris Knowles High School   1968

Emphasizes how she functioned as a buyer.

Chemist/Manager   Functional

John C. Morrison, Jr.
34 Candear Street
Tampa, Florida 33675
813-724-2116

MANAGEMENT   Planned, budgeted and managed development of products
                    from inception through final production. Hired, developed
                    and supervised achievement-oriented professionals and
                    technicians. Organized and coordinated teams of R&D,
                    marketing and market research people for key projects,
                    and established procedures for managing and controlling
                    projects.

TECHNICAL   Achieved technical and consumer objectives for innovative
                    underarm products, facial cleansers and hand lotions.
                    Solved critical problems in formulating, packaging and
                    evaluating performance of anhydrous suspension roll on,
                    pump, aerosol and squeeze spray deodorants. Supervised
                    manufacture, microbiological, safety and efficacy testing
                    of products. Directed research in dry skin treatment,
                    including developing instrumental methods for evaluating
                    product actions.

                    Invented processes for surface coloring gelatin capsules
                    and spray-granulating powders. Developed electronically
                    instrumented tablet presses and an electronic method
                    for measuring antiperspirant activity. Created novel
                    shampoos, rinses, shaving aids, foot sprays, contact
                    lens solutions, plus dentifrice, antiseptic, cold, and
                    vitamin preparations.

COMMUNICATIONS   Maintained R&D liaison with marketing, market research,
                    advertising, legal and regulatory agencies. Presented
                    key accomplishment and progress reports to senior technical
                    and business management. Handled technical training pro-
                    grams for sales, marketing and advertising people and
                    prepared comprehensive safety and efficacy manuals to
                    obtain management clearance for sale of products. Inter-
                    faced with contract manufacturers, consulting and testing
                    laboratories.

EMPLOYMENT   1974 - Present Chemical and Metal Products, Tampa,
                                    Florida, Group Leader
                    1971 - 1974   Hobson & Hobson, Fort Lauderdale, Fla.,
                                    Group Leader
                    1955 - 1971   Extensive product and process development
                                    experience in various ethical proprietary
                                    pharmaceuticals, toiletries and cosmetic
                                    products.

EDUCATION   B.S. (Pharmacy) Albany College of Pharmacy, Union
                    University. Additional courses in pharmaceutical and
                    cosmetic engineering, aerosol technology, improving
                    managerial skills.

De-emphasizes frequent job changes.

Copywriter   Functional

MANDY MILES

450 West End Avenue
New York, New York 10023
(212) 787-1993

Writing-Freelance

. Wrote twelve article series on personal development, fashion and
  home furnishings for Co-Ed magazine.
. Wrote feature articles for Ingenue magazine.
. Created home-sewing shows for Co-Ed given in major department
  stores across the country.
. Co-authored paperback book on teenage problems for Pentamex
  Publications.

Film Strip Production

. Produced "Loving Relationships" - a half hour film strip for
  high school students for Co-Ed. Wrote "Beautiful Foods" filmstrip
  for Co-Ed.
. Edited over 50 filmstrips for use by high schools in area of music,
  art history and literature for Bramston Publications.

Fund-Raising

. Assumed major responsibilities in scholarship fund-raising efforts.
. Created craft projects and directed weekly workshops which pro-
  duced hundreds of items for large handcrafts bazaar.
. Organized theatrical and cultural benefits.

Work History

1975-Present	Major fundraising projects	
1969-1975	Freelance Writing assignments	
1967-1969	Ideas for Youth	Editor
	Parameter Publications	

. Wrote articles, produced photography, supervised art.

1963-1967	Co-Ed magazine	Fashion Editor

. Covered fashion Markets; supervised photography, art, layout,
  wrote copy; produced fashion show.
. Received award for editorial excellence from American Institute of
  Men's and Boy's Wear

1962-1963	Anik Robelin-Paris	Designer's Assistant

Education

1962	B.A. Art History/English U.C.L.A.

Being in an artistic field, Mandy can be bolder in her design.

Data Processing

Functional

Joan M. Cabrillo
2280 Bal Harbor Drive
Miami, Florida 33154
(305) 274-8096

Supervisory   Supervised 2 IBM 360/30 systems with input/output
               devices comprising six 2311 desk storage drives,
               four 2401 11 tape drives, two 2540 card reader and
               two 1403 printers. Exercised full supervisory
               authority over two supervisors and a staff of
               25-computer operators, keypunch operators and control
               clerks. As supervisor of script stock, directed
               activities of a staff of 40.

Data Processing   Formulated mathematical models of systems, set up
                   controls analog and hybrid computer system to solve
                   scientific and engineering problems. Computed vol-
                   tage and time scales to convert mathematical equations
                   into computer equations to obtain potentiometer set-
                   tings.

                   Drew computer circuit diagrams to indicate connec-
                   tions between components and their values. Observed
                   behavior of variables on output devices such as plot-
                   ters, recorders, digital voltmeters, oscilliscopes,
                   digital displays and readouts to obtain solutions.

Work History:

1973 - present   IBM Corporation - Supervisor of Script Stock

1971 - 73   F.S. Smith & Co. - Operations Dept. Supervisor

1964 - 71   Tromson & McKannon - Supervisor of Computer Room

Education:

1979   B.S. Degree expected - Miami Dade College

1976   Miami Community College - Computer Science

1973   University of Florida Programming Design and Analysis

1969   IBM Education Center

1960   Electronic Computer Programming Institute

Language: COBOL

College student. Emphasizes functions of jobs *and* training.

Electrical Engineer

Tim Chow-Chu
792 Ocean Avenue
Arlington, Virginia 22212
703-883-9763

Targeted

Job Target: Electrical Engineer - Research and Development

CAPABILITIES:

- Conduct R & D concerning design, manufacture and testing of electrical components, equipment and systems
- Apply new uses to equipment
- Design manufacturing, construction and installation procedures
- Direct staff of engineering personnel in producing test control equipment
- Direct test programs to insure conformance of equipment and systems to customer requirements
- Direct and coordinate field installations

ACHIEVEMENTS:

- I have designed and drafted ship, vessel electrical deck plans including power, lighting and systems and security.
- I have designed, drafted and tested telephone relay wirings, alarm and security systems circuitry.
- I have done calculations in accord with the latest N.E. Code together with the best economic and engineering considerations.
- I have designed and done layout of plans, sections and details of power distribution, systems and security.
- I have designed and done layout of H.V.A.C. wirings and control wiring diagrams.

Work History

1973-Present	Rosenblatt, Inc. - Junior Electrical Engineer
1972-1973	Smith-Abbot, Inc. - Electrical Designer
1969-72	National Telephone - Engineering Aide
1967-69	Electrical Draftsman

Education

Catholic University - Washington, D.C. - 1972 B.S. Electrical Engineering
IES - 1975 - Course in Commercial and Industrial Lighting Design
National Taiwan University - Taipei, Taiwan 1963 B.A. Business
Administration.

Doesn't emphasize frequent job changes.

Die Designer   Chronological

Fred M. April
2240 Ponet Drive
Los Angeles, California   90068
213-467-4872

PROFESSIONAL EXPERIENCE

1973-Present   Motor Coaches, Inc., Santa Monica, California

Die Designer   Responsible for design of small progressive dies to
                produce ends for metal cans. Participated in design
                of Button Down and Stay-on Tab ends.

                Researched complete end die project for Indonesia,
                resulting in substantial savings due to prevention
                of manufacturing redundant and obsolete parts.

                Designed tooling for manufacture of plastic tops for
                Dixie Cup Division.

1971-1973   Watson-Edison Company, Pacific Palisades, California

Designer   Designed conveyor layout for plant. Designed struc-
                tural platforms and rings, floor layout for install-
                ation of presses, hoppers and other heavy equipment.
                Designed carbon-air batteries for use on railroads
                and buoys. Designed small fixtures to speed up and
                ease assembly line production.

1970-1971   Motor Coaches, Inc., Santa Monica, California

Design   Designed can closing machine hook-ups to fillers;
Draftsman   layout work on presses and dies. Designed open end
                detector used on can closing machines to detect
                incomplete curled end seams after cans are sealed.

1961-1970   Yardley Electric Corporation, Los Angeles, California

Designer   Designed three silver-cell batteries for use in aero-
                space systems. Participated in the design of the
                "Hamilton Standard" battery used in the backpack of
                astronauts to maintain temperature in space suit.

                Technical illustrating and poster work, most notably
                30" x 40" color renderings of two Air-Zinc batteries
                designed for the U.S. Army Signal Corps and cover
                illustrations for the Company pamphlet distributed at
                the I.R.E. show.

EDUCATION

1962-1963   Los Angeles Community College
1960-1962   Delehanty Drafting Institute
1952-1954   UCLA

Design Engineer

Jim S. Pedusky
31 Lookout Street
Cranford, New Jersey 07405
(201) 838-9084

Chronological

EXPERIENCE

1970 - 1978.   Eight years experience in mechanical design engineering.

Design Engineer, Industrial Metal Company

Contributed significantly to the design and development
of the firm's metal products. Assumed the responsibilities
of putting prototype products into commercial production,
maintaining a budget, and meeting deadlines. This included
the design (layouts) and development of high-speed transfer
presses, roll forming machinery, assembly machinery, and
associated tooling, gages, feed mechanisms, and controls.
Tooling included progressive dies, compound dies, deep
draw dies, and precision coining and embossing dies.

Demonstrated the ability to lead designers, detailers,
and machine shop personnel on major projects, and dealt
with customers and vendors.

Member of the engineering center "Computer Use Committee."
Responsible for the choice and research of new programming.

1968 - 1970.   Mechanical Technician, Industrial Metal Company

Main function was debugging and modifying new equipment.
Toward the end of this period, successfully directed
efforts to the development of new metal products.

1966 - 1968.   Machinist and Toolmaker, L & R Mechanical Laboratory,
Wayne, New Jersey.

Performed all facets in the making of precision tools and
gages. Experienced the programming and set up of numerical
control machines.

1964.   Machinist, Bowles Engineering Company.

Performed basic machining on many types of components and
machines.

EDUCATION

1975 - Present. Fairleigh Dickinson University. 110 credits with high
academic standing (3.82 out of possible 4.0)

Executive Secretary   Targeted

DEBORAH K. MAXELL
220 W. E Street
Washington, D.C. 20009
202-998-7236

JOB TARGET: EXECUTIVE SECRETARY TO PRESIDENT

Capabilities:

*Create and maintain a simple, highly workable file system.
*Supervise office staff.
*Handle high-pressure phone calls.
*Compose and prepare routine correspondence.
*Prepare financial and other reports.
*Handle purchasing for large office.
*Handle travel and hotel arrangements.
*Manage social as well as business correspondence.

Achievements:

*Managed business relationships with high level financial
 executives.
*Supervised staff including assistant, receptionist,
 steward, and wire operator.
*Assisted with daily cash placement.
*Planned itineraries, arranged trips.
*Assisted editing of financial reports.
*Maintained business and personal calendars.
*Took dictation.
*Arranged installation of electronic quotation equipment
 for 100 branch offices.
*Arranged bank loans for firm officers.

Work history:

1975-Present   AZOR CORPORATION - Executive Secretary
               to Vice President, Finance

1974-75   GENERAL SECURITIES CORPORATION - Executive
               Secretary and Personal Secretary to Vice
               President

1967-74   JASON-WALKER INC. - Executive Secretary to
               Executive Vice President

Education:

1974 Bentley Business Systems.
S.U.N.Y. Buffalo
New York Institute of Finance

Emphasizes capabilities, not experience. Colleges listed but not dated, as there were no actual
degrees.

Hospital Administrator   Targeted

NED MILES
14 Rosewood Lane
Garden City, New York 11530
516-737-7280

JOB TARGET: HOSPITAL ADMINISTRATOR

CAPABILITIES:

* Handle in-depth coordinating and planning
* Direct complex activities in operations and finance
* Contribute to hospitals, health care facilities, HIP, Fortune 500
  industrial and commercial corporations
* Manage commercial medical administration for headquarters as
  well as divisions
* Act as coordinating liaison among diverse groups
* Establish and maintain excellent budget reports

ACHIEVEMENTS:

* Developed and implemented policies and procedures for eight
  medical centers serving 125,000 HIP subscribers.
* Recruited and hired administrative staff for eight centers.
* Assisted Chief Administrator in training program preparation.
* Prepared and maintained capital project status and budget re-
  ports for New York City's 18 hospitals and care centers.
* Communicated directly with Executive Directors.
* Acted as liaison officer with contractors, vendors, department
  heads interrelating with medical staff regarding their needs.
* Coordinated multi-shop activities for a major health care complex.
* Established an on-site office for a major missile producer.
* Recruited, trained and directed employees responsible for
  stocking missile site with capital equipment spare parts.

WORK EXPERIENCE:

1974-Present	Pan Borough Hospital Center	Maintenance Control Planner
1971-1974	La Juania Medical Group	Administrative Coordinator
1970-1971	New York City Hospitals Corp.	Planning Analyst
1969-1970	New York University Hospital	AD. ASST-Director of Engineering
1952-1969	Various Corporate Gov't Contracts	Project Planner

EDUCATION:

| 1950 | Columbia University |

Emphasize expanded capabilities. De-emphasize frequent job changes.

Lawyer

Functional

SHARON HARTLEY KALEN

340 West End Avenue
New York, N.Y. 10024
(212) 595-4240

EXPERIENCE

Litigation: Extensive attainments in all phases of civil litigation in State and Federal Courts; successfully conducted depositions and trials in a variety of media and commercial cases; achieved notable results through expertise in State and Federal Court brief-writing; reduced costs through self-training and management of department in creditors' rights and bankruptcy cases; achieved favorable resolution of complex, difficult-to-win cases through meticulous work and incisive deployment of strategies; practiced before administrative boards and arbitrators.

Media: Voluminous practice in all aspects of media law for large and medium-sized clients; expertly conducted and directed media litigations; avoided litigation through creative merging of legal and editorial skills in prepublishing libel and privacy counseling; analyzed and managed copyright and corporate matters; planned and negotiated contracts and settlements.

Management: Skilled in perceptive direction of research, planning of trial and pretrial strategy; reduced unnecessary time spent by others on work projects through careful supervision of work; maintained extensive client contact; selected, supervised and controlled local counsel in out-of-state cases to assure highest results while avoiding large billings.

EMPLOYMENT HISTORY

Balmer, Kaye, Saams & Hartman, 200 Park Avenue, New York, N.Y. 1970 to date. Senior Associate.

EDUCATION

Columbia Law School, LLB Cum Laude, 1969
Harlan Fiske Stone Scholar; Dean's List.

Columbia College, B.A. 1966
Top 10% of Class; Dean's List.

PUBLICATIONS

Columbia Journal of Law and Social Problems. Editor.
Kings Crown Essays. Managing Editor.

Librarian   Functional

ALICIA SHERMAN
170-72 Melbourne Street
Jackson Heights, New York 11328
212-791-8037

LIBRARY CONSULTING

Revised and edited author catalogue. Verified entries in
bibliographic sources. Set up outreach program that resulted
in 30% greater use of library. Conducted senior citizens seminars that included extensive use of audiovisual materials.
Handled book selection and ordering. Processed gift books
and film programming. Developed and administered high school
English language library.

LIBRARY RESEARCH & REFERENCE

Handled extensive reference work in social and behavioral sciences.
Trained numerous small groups in use of reference sources such
as card or book catalogue or book and periodical indexes to
locate information. Demonstrated procedures for searching
catalogue files. Serviced government documents. Maintained
vertical and curriculum files as well as film programs and
book reviewing.

WORK EXPERIENCE:

1978   AMERICAN MUSEUM OF ANCIENT HISTORY LIBRARY   Consultant

1972-77 QUEENSBOROUGH PUBLIC LIBRARY, Flushing Branch Librarian

PUBLICATIONS:

Author Catalogue; American Museum of Ancient History for their
library. Jewish American and their History: Sources--- American
Library Association.

AFFILIATIONS:

American Library Association

EDUCATION:

Master Library Science, 1974; B.A. in History, 1971 Queens College

Spotty work history is not emphasized.

Manager, Business

Robert C. White
87 South Columbia Avenue
White Plains, NY 10604
(914) 883-8052

Functional

MANAGEMENT: Hired telephone consultant engineers and trained them in
                   technical and interpersonal communications. Successfully
                   expanded this group from 3 to 15. Developed career path
                   strategy and created charts with management for levels of
                   telephone consultant to project engineer.

TRAINING: In a 10 month period trained over 150 people--senior
                   executives, critical care area managers, salesmen and
                   field engineers. Established task analysis and course
                   objectives for these trainees. Applied critical judgement
                   and professional competence in instructing over 150
                   field personnel in various locations.

ADMINISTRATION: Handled inventory of technical education department.
                   Organized information for budget and delivered to manage-
                   ment. Supervised small group responsible for maintaining
                   logistics for telephone central operations. Developed
                   telephone call sheet formats which were later fed into a
                   computer resulting in failure analysis reports now used
                   nationally.

TECHNICAL: Responsible for instruction on mini and micro computer-
                   controlled biomedical instrumentation. Developed trouble-
                   shooting procedures and charts on assigned instrumentation
                   for customer and field service manuals. Served as national
                   technical backup to service engineers on existing and
                   developmental instrumentation. Performed the operational
                   maintenance, troubleshooting, repair, retrofit and updating
                   of in-house production and customer education instrumenta-
                   tion. Quality control inspector for repair group under my
                   supervision.

1972--PRESENT   Technical Products Corporation

Started in loan and repair department and worked through the technical ranks
to current position of Technical Instructor.

EDUCATION: Technician Certificate, 1972 Electronics Certificate, 1969
                  Current--Westchester Community College Electrical Engineering

Emphasize management functions; not emphasize current job title.

Manager/Executive   Chronological

Marcia S. Lohman
421 E. Haley Street
Philadelphia, Pennsylvania 19146
215-234-7988

Executive Vice President Management, Vice President Programs for Employers
IMPETUS - Philadelphia, Pennsylvania
October 73-Present

Managed all administrative operations. Directed the work of five
functional units. Active in formulation and implementation of organizational policy. Planned, developed and evaluated programs and
publications. Developed and designed programs and materials. Prepared brochures and other promotional material to increase sales.

Corporate Director of Operations
NATIONAL RESEARCH & DEVELOPMENT CORPORATION - Philadelphia, Pennsylvania
January 1966-October 1973

Managed all educational and manpower projects. Assisted project
directors in all technical management functions. Prepared proposals
for both private and public funding sources. Negotiated contracts.
Evaluated on-site operations to insure effective implementation of
contractual requirements.

Director of Research, Office of Inspection
OFFICE OF ECONOMICS - City of New York
March 1965-January 1966

Organized and maintained an "early warning system" to identify
local community action problems for agency director. Coordinated
national inspection visits. Prepared research reports for the
agency's Congressional presentation.

1960-1965   Various research positions - New York

EDUCATION:

Miami University, Oxford, Ohio   1959
B.A. - Honors in English

Manager, Insurance   Functional

Robert M. Bradley
72 Meadows Rd.
Southfield, Michigan 48037
313-279-8809

MANAGEMENT: Responsible for day to day smooth operation of home
                     office. Hired and trained personnel in selling
                     insurance and processing claims. Reviewed activity
                     reports for status of sales quotas, underwriting, and
                     crediting collections to accounts. Developed sales
                     methods leading to 60% sales increase in nine months.
                     Reconciled commission accounts for salespersons.

SALES: Sold insurance to 20 new major accounts in six
                     months. Sold increased insurance to over one dozen
                     present customers. Analyzed insurance require-
                     ments for over 100 prospective clients. Supervised
                     ten salespersons; trained them in sales techniques
                     resulting in a 60% increase in sales.

UNDERWRITING: Processed risks ranging from small $5,000 single
                     engine aircraft to large multiengine $30 million
                     commercial jets. Increased territorial premium
                     volume 20%. Revised underwriting manual: developed
                     new claims forms; set up underwriting training
                     program.

WORK HISTORY:

1973-present   Associated Aeronautics Underwriters
                        Manager of Office Services
                        Underwriter
                        Assistant Underwriter
                        Special Agent

1967-1973   U.S. Air Force
                        Pilot
                        Operations Officer
                        Squadron Commander

EDUCATION:

College of Insurance   1968
Stevens Institute of Technology   1967
General Engineering

Making a move into management from supervisor.

Manager/Technical   Targeted

Ward Gantney
250 Fort Salonga Road
Northport, New York 11687
(516) 725-5286

JOB TARGET: Management Position in Materials Science, instrument applications
             or instrument sales.

CAPABILITIES:

  *Write, edit and approve professional reports.
  *Provide consultation and support to U.S. Government on contamination problems.
  *Set up procedures and special techniques for the nondestructive analysis
     of integrated circuits, printed circuit boards, semi-conductor devices,
     laser materials and inertial components.
  *Organize and maintain analytical facilities for the characterization of
     metals, alloys, ceramics, polymers, plastics, fluids and lubricants.
  *Manage programs in materials and component development
  *Conduct corrosion and outgassing studies.

ACHIEVEMENTS:

  *Supervised analytical chemistry lab of 6-9 graduate chemists
  *Acted as trouble shooter for equipment failure associated with aerospace
     and ocean systems
  *Purchased all technical equipment
  *Set up non-destructive testing procedures for failure analysis of
     integrated circuits.
  *Conducted comparative analysis of surfactants in electroplated and
     anodized parts.
  *Assisted in developing procedure for removing carbon inclusions from
     diamonds.

WORK HISTORY:

  1951 - Present   Gage-West Corp.   Supervisor, Analytical Chemistry Lab
  1975-6   Darnell Electronics   Consultant
  1974-76   RET Surface Chemicals   Consultant

EDUCATION:

  Hofstra University   1952 M.A. Microbiology, Oceanography
                       1950 B.A. Chemistry
  Long Island Univ.   Business Administration 1966

Emphasize capabilities for a move upward.

Market Analyst/Researcher   Chronological

ROBERT M. GORMAN, C.F.A.

53 Rutgers Drive
Port Washington, New York   11050
(516) 882-5082

1968-Present   W.B. WHITNEY & COMPANY   New York, New York

Electrical/Electronic Analyst. Follow the major
appliance, consumer electronic, and electronic
component industries. Analyze companies and
industries, and evaluate stocks. Handle numerous
clients such as banks, mutual funds and insurance
companies. Discuss findings, predict market trends
and advise clients on sensitive issues.

1962-1968   IMC DIVISION OF MRW, INC.   Philadelphia, Pennsylvania

Market Research Manager. Supervised two analysts
and performed studies on the market for fixed and
variable resistors in the television, computer,
automotive and other electronic markets. Fore-
casted annual industry demand for company's products.
Evaluated potential acquisitions. Chairman of
Electronic Industries Association Resistor Marketing
Committee.

1956-1962   WOLMITE TRANSISTOR DIVISION OF WOLMITE CORP.
                                        Waltham, Massachusetts

Market Research Manager. Identified applications
and markets of various semi-conductor technologies.
Evaluated potential markets and monitored trends
in the computer, power rectifier, television, automotive and instrumentation markets.

Senior Engineer. Designed high current rectifier
test equipment and trained customers on rectifier
applications.

Electronic Engineer & Physicist. Worked in various
departments of Wolmite, Inc. and the University of
Pennsylvania Physics Department.

AFFILIATIONS: Institute of Chartered Financial Analysts; IEEE
                   New York Society of Security Analysts

EDUCATION: M.A. Wesleyan University
                   B.S. Northeastern University in Electrical Engineering

Marketing Manager   Targeted

DAVID C. HALPERN
6200 Pershing Road
Chicago, Illinois 60609
(312) 569-0917

JOB TARGET: *SALES OR MARKETING MANAGEMENT WITH AN INTERNATIONAL*
CORPORATION LEADING TO SENIOR MANAGEMENT RESPONSIBILITY

CAPABILITIES:

* Market and sell industrial and agricultural chemicals
* Direct and coordinate activities concerned with research and
  development of new concepts, ideas, and basic data on an organization's products, services or ideologies
* Plan and formulate aspects of research and development proposals, such as purpose of project, applications to be utilized
  from findings, cost of project and equipment and manpower
  requirements
* Approve and submit proposals considered feasible to management
  for consideration and allocation of funds
* Develop and implement methods and procedures for monitoring
  projects such as project reports and staff conferences
* Negotiate contracts with consulting firms to perform studies
* Achieve competitive edge through effective use of know-how
  in product coordination, ship chartering, insurance and letters
  of credit

ACHIEVEMENTS:

* Managed cost analyses pertinent to specific products and
  countries in relation to total consumption, pricing, competitors, market share, local production facilities, freighting
  and credit.
* Successfully gained market information through agents, distri-
  butors, and international government agencies.
* Arranged sensitive off-shore deals and "swap-out material" with
  competitors in Europe, the Far East and Latin America.
* Sold industrial packaging materials to numerous Fortune 500
  corporations.
* Increased market share of an industrial paper product from
  27% to 31% in six month period.

WORK HISTORY:

1974-present	INTERNATIONAL CHEMICALS & SUBSTANCES CORPORATION	
	Trading Division	Trader
	Chemical Group	Product Manager
1971-1974	CROWN ZELLERBACH CORPORATION	
	Industrial Packaging	Sales Representative
1965-1971	AMERICAN EXPORT SHIPPING	Vessel Navigator

EDUCATION: Stanford University   M.B.A. International Business 1974

Expanded job target. Allows to develop capabilities.

Nutritionist   Functional

ALICE KASIELEWICZ

123 Burgum Hall, NDSU - Present   405 First Avenue Northwest - Permanent
Fargo, ND 58105   Little Falls, MN 56345
(701) 237-8329 or 241-2073   (612) 632-5687

EDUCATION

North Dakota State University, B.S. 1979. Major: Administrative Dietetics,
Minor: Business

EXPERIMENTAL METHODS AND RESEARCH
. Devised and carried out experiments in advanced food classes.
. Operated an assortment of precise laboratory measuring equipment.
. Wrote results and reported orally experimental findings.
. Designed experiment varying the oil in chiffon cakes.

RECIPE DEVELOPMENT AND MENU PLANNING
. Had a major role in development of the Cooking with Pictures project.
. Formulated and tested recipes in class and field evaluations.
. Critiqued and evaluated a variety of recipes.
. Assisted in creating the layouts and printing for recipes.
. Organized and edited promotional material in preparation for sales.
. Extensive experience in developing menus and market orders.
. Analyzed nutritional requirements for all age levels and food preferences.

FOOD PREPARATION
. Extensive experience in baking (with and without mixes) breads, cakes,
  and cookies for hundreds of people.
. Strong familiarity with all basic principles of food preparation.
. Have prepared complete, balanced and appetizing meals in quantities.
. Much work with home and commercial food preparation equipment.

FOODSERVICE MANAGEMENT
. Management of summer foodservice activities for 30 fraternity residents.
. Supervised all aspects of foodservice for a special weekend project
  during NDSU's Upward Bound program.
. Directed meal preparation for mentally handicapped residents.
. Took charge of all summer food procurement and preparation at Camp Watson.

EMPLOYMENT:

1976-1979   Dr. Bettie Stanislao, Food and Nutrition Department, NDSU
     1978   Resident Dining Center, Auxiliary Enterprizes, NDSU
     1978   Farmhouse Fraternity and Upward Bound at NDSU
     1977   Mr. Vern Lindsay, Camp Director, Children's Village Family Service

COMMUNITY ACTIVITIES AND ORGANIZATIONS:

Involved in a variety of organizations including a Tasting Committee, Student
Dietetic Association, Senior Citizen Nutrition Programs, and participated in a
research project entitled "The Food Preservation Practices of North Dakota."

A college student capitalizing on extracurricular activities.

Personnel Supervisor

Functional

DANIEL N. CUONO
36 Royal Crest Dr.
Nashua, New Hampshire 03060
(603) 246-9876

COMMUNICATION/
MANAGEMENT

Responsible for project interviews, staffing and maintaining of in-house accounts. Supervised all levels of technical personnel and projects for clients such as Pratt & Whitney, Pfaudler, Permutit and Reeves Instrument. Evaluated personnel; conducted training programs; established wage incentives.

Directed and supervised technical personnel for completion of design proposal. Assisted sales staff in developing proposals for customers. Assisted the shop in solving manufacturing and assembly problems.

PUBLIC
RELATIONS

Handled engineering problems in public relations with U.S. clients such as Mobil Oil, Hormel and Quaker Oats, and Canadian clients: Molson Brewery and Campbell Soup Company.

Maintained engineering liaison with other companies furnishing support for customer's filler closing machine systems. Designed an integrated filler/closing system for customers. Represented Consolidated Sheet Metal Company at customer's plant for start up, trouble shooting, debugging and evaluation.

DESIGN/
DEVELOPMENT

Developed new designs or modifications for closing machines, ham press, cheese block wrapper, as well as other can packaging equipment. Considered by Company as expert on 24 models of closing machines.

EMPLOYMENT HISTORY

1966 - Present	Consolidated Sheet Metal Company Nashua, New Hampshire	Design Engineer
1951 - 1966	Designers & Consultants New York City	Project Supervisor

Total career change. De-emphasize engineering function.

Photographer   Functional

Margaret Sawhill
106 W. University Parkway
Baltimore, Maryland 21210
(301) 655-3178

MAJOR WORK EXPERIENCE

Photography   Staff photographer for magazine. Designed setup
for and photographed food products. Covered trade
convention personnel and equipment. Photographed
restaurant interiors and institutional equipment.
Shot outdoor scenics and nature closeups. Photographed how-to series on construction projects.
food preparation, and maintenance. Illustrated
articles on interior decoration. Taught basic
photography to salesmen.

Writing   Researched and wrote scientific articles in fields
of chemistry, mathematics, and physics. Converted
scientific data into layman's language. Researched
and developed articles on industrial equipment,
plastics, and food service. Wrote instruction
manuals on data processing procedures.

Editing   Edited technical and semi-technical manuscripts in
science field. Solicited authors for technical
articles. Edited trade magazine copy. Made
layouts and dummied pages. Free-lance-edited science
books.

EMPLOYERS   Edifice Magazine - Staff photographer, assistant
editor

Miami Academy of Sciences - Associate editor

Garbier, Inc. - Science editor

EDUCATION   Miami University, B.A.
Maryland Institute of Art - Non-credit courses in painting

Left out dates of employers, as her most *recent* job was as keypunch operator.

Program Developer   Chronological

AGATHA WHITEHEAD
6450 Lindell Blvd.
St. Louis, Missouri 63110
(314) 752-3438

CONFERENCE AND SEMINAR MANAGEMENT

1975-present   As DIRECTOR OF PROGRAM DEVELOPMENT for Washington University School of
Continuing Education, designed and staffed 40 programs focused on business
and career development. Redesigned the career program to include:
personnel management, basic and advanced career workshops, arts management, communication skills for secretaries, fundraising and grantsmanship,
fundamentals of marketing.

Managerial and administrative responsibilities include: Course conceptual-
ization and design, faculty hiring and salary negotiation, administrative
staff supervision, brochure design, scheduling, coordination of direct
mail, advertising, public relations, location selection and space ne-
negotiation.

1973-75   PROGRAM PRODUCER/HOST WNAL-FM, CLAYTON, MISSOURI

Originated VOICES, a weekly radio show focused on human development and
public affairs. Topics included: career and life planning, women and
management, EEO, Title IX, book and film discussion and reviews, job
satisfaction, adult life stages and the quality of work life.

Production and administrative responsibilities included: research of
topics, development of discussion formats, selection and scheduling of
guests, promotion on air and off and interviewing.

1969-73   HUMANITIES INSTRUCTOR, CLAYTON CENTRAL SCHOOL DISTRICT

Improved student performance and teacher accountability. Developed and
implemented innovative learning contracts incorporating needs assessment,
performance objectives and joint student-teacher evaluation procedures.

Trained staff in individualized learning methods. Organized and coordinated
a symposium on Futuristics and a community Ethnic Festival now held every
year. Improved communications as a liaison among schools, Humanities
departments and communities via direct mail, large and small group
presentations and audio-visual programs on various topics.

EDUCATION: St. Louis University   B.A. 1969
             St. Louis University   M.A. in progress
             Recent course work in Video and Film Production at the New School, N.Y.
             Seminars and conferences in Management, Organization Development, Human
             Resources and Training.

Public Relations   Functional

WILLIAM J. ALBRECHT
84 Westfield Rd.
Richmond, Virginia 23203
804-988-7709

PUBLIC RELATIONS   Handled customer complaints in large retail
                     store. Organized employee-employer liaison
                     group and represented employee views to
                     management. Conducted interviews with prom-
                     inent sports figures for publication in local
                     paper. Successfully negotiated language and
                     living relationships in Switzerland. Acted
                     as spokesman for college track team.

SALES   Sold merchandise in nationally known de-
                     partment store. Handled three times pre-
                     vious volume in sales. Produced high sales
                     of six previously slow-moving items. Trained
                     three other successful salespersons.

ACCOUNTING   Handled all bookkeeping and accounting for
                     local retail store. Prepared payroll, wrote
                     checks, made reports. Supervised all pur-
                     chases, reduced incidental expenses by 30%.

Experience

1979 to Present   MADE IN AMERICA STORE - Bookkeeper

1976-79   E.J. KORVETTE - Salesperson

1974   CIBA-GEIGY CORPORATION - Shipping Clerk

Education

1979   B.A. English   University of Virginia

Specialties

9 months living in Switzerland
Proficiency in reading, writing and speaking French.

Note the career shift.

Rehabilitative Physiotherapist   Targeted

Jackson F. Gardner
7142 Hickory Dr.
Seville, Colorado 81009
303-249-7269

Job Target: Rehabilitative Physiotherapist

Abilities:
- Determine appropriate treatment for muscular injuries
- Accurately diagnose sprains, strains and ruptures
- Prepare detailed home care programs
- Train loss-of-limb patients in use and care of prosthetic devices
- Provoke motivation in newly handicapped patients
- Train medical personnel in basics of physical therapy
- Accurately evaluate physician's recommendations
- Administer therapy by light, heat, water and electricity
- Effectively use ultrasound and diathermy equipment

Accomplishments:
- Diagnosed and treated hundreds of patients successfully
- Performed extensive patient tests and evaluations such as - range of motion, functional analyses and body parts measurements
- Administered a variety of massage techniques, deep and superficial
- Administered traction equipment to patients
- Prepared accurate records of patient treatment and progress
- Fitted patients with orthotics
- Trained patients in manual therapeutic exercises for home care
- Assisted patients in adjusting daily activities to support their condition

Work History: 1977-Present   St. Mary's Hospital - Colorado Staff Physical Therapist

                      1977   University of Illinois Medical Center Intern Physical Therapist

Education: Certificate of Physical Therapy 1977
                      University of Michigan
                      B.S. - Physical Therapy 1977

Retail Management   Chronological

Robert B. Green
420 York Avenue □ New York City 10021 □ (212) 628-1815 □ Ans. Svc. (516) 766-2211

**Bloomingdale's
1976 to Present**

RETAIL MANAGEMENT ...

At Bloomingdale's, assisted in managing all facets of the New York Department's business and supervised the operations of nine Branch Store Departments. Managed twelve salespersons, handled customer relations, accounts payable functions, inventory control, and merchandise flow through traffic and receiving departments. Total stock responsibilities 1.4 million dollars.

MERCHANDISING ...

As Assistant Buyer, developed two significant areas of business. Introduced a relatively unknown line of merchandise. Determined proper assortment, designed advertising campaign and obtained $20,000 in allowances from the manufacturer. New line resulted in $24,000 increase over previous year with substantial future projection. Created "Christmas shops" for key merchandise in the New York Store and all Branches. Personally monitored and balanced stock daily to maximize profits. Generated a 50% sales increase above preceding year.

SALES TRAINING ...

Developed a Video Training program at Bloomingdale's used in branch stores for new department managers and sales people. Formal programs were extremely effective tools, affording the participant a thorough understanding of the products supported with current information and sales techniques.

**University of
Cincinnati (Ohio)**

PROMOTION AND PUBLIC RELATIONS ...

Produced distinguished lecture series at the University of Cincinnati. Personally negotiated and directed a campaign to have a figure of extreme national interest speak at the University. Worked closely with Cincinnati Public Information Center. Coordinated national and local press conference, handled all contract negotiations, arranged promotion, all public relations with community and press, box office arrangements, and hospitality for speakers. Supervised staff of 25.

**College Marketing
Research Corp.**

MARKET RESEARCH

Conducted studies in the Cincinnati area for the College Marketing Research Corporation, a division of Playboy Enterprises, involving the distribution of thirty major publications and paperback publishers. Results: Improved circulation of books and magazine. Supervised staff of 15.

**Warner Brothers
(Record Division)**

PHOTOGRAPHY ...

Covered major musical events in the New York and Cincinnati areas for Warner Brothers Records (free lance).

Education

University of Cincinnati (Ohio)
Bachelor of Fine Arts -- June 1976
Major: Communications   Minor: Business Administration

**Honors and
Activities**

Dean's List	Student Program Board
Student Speakers Bureau—Chairman	WFIB Radio—Music Director
Presidents Advisory Board	News Record—Staff
National Entertainment Conference	

Robert's job target allows him to be more adventurous in use of typesetting.

Sales/Retail   # Functional

Cynthia Connelly
36 Waverly Court
Alamo, California 94507
213-682-3177

SALES/RETAIL   Managed over one hundred East Coast
                        accounts for large West Coast Gourmet
                        Club. Developed promotional campaigns
                        for new product lines. Increased sales
                        by $500,000 in nine month period. Co-
                        ordinated accounts of over 20 large
                        department stores. Sold specialty
                        clothing for West Coast shop dealing
                        with special and difficult clients.

MANAGEMENT   Organized and implemented a program for
                        forty college students abroad. Co-
                        ordinated student-faculty liaison
                        relationship. Managed an inventory
                        of several thousand items. Trained
                        and supervised 3 assistants.

WRITING   Wrote several free-lance articles published
                        in a California daily. Composed cor-
                        respondence in French as well as English.
                        Fluent reading, writing and speaking
                        French, Spanish and Italian.

                        Experience

1976 - Present   COQ AU VIN GOURMET CLUB
                        Promotional Sales

1976   PINK PUSSYCAT BOUTIQUE
                        Salesperson

                        Education

1976   UC at Berkeley B.A.

Cynthia's job title was not impressive, but her accomplishments were, so she used the functional format.

Secretary   Chronological

SANDRA GRUEN
208 S. Broad Street
New Orleans, Louisiana 70183
504-456-9923

Experience

1976-Present   GENERAL PACKAGING CO.   Technical Secretary

Handled technical typing for department of nine.
Composed correspondence and shipping forms. Organized and maintained over 350 files. Recorded
shipments sent in and prepared shipping forms
for samples being sent out. Achieved monetary
saving by eliminating purchase of stencils and
ink.

1974-1976   GERBEL ENGINEERING CORPORATION   Bookkeeper

Processed accounts receivable checks for real
estate properties. Paid real estate taxes,
insurance premiums and utilities for real estate.
Prepared financial statements. Organized and
submitted monthly reports. Prepaid insurance
premiums. Typed yearly financial statements for
corporation.

1972   SALVATION ARMY   Office Manager

Supervised office functions, including supplies
purchasing, clerical functions. Raised $260,000
for new community center. Set up office--designed
forms, prepared news releases, letters and
acknowledgements. Recorded donations and pledges
made by corporations, organizations, and individuals.

Education   Professional School for Business, New Orleans,
Louisiana: Real Estate

Sandra stayed with chronological, as she was keeping the same job target.

Securities Analyst   Chronological

JOSHUA A. MARGOLIS
72 Beuer Court
Cambridge, Massachusetts 02140
617-247-8299

1967-Present	ARNOLD BURNHAM & CO. Boston, Massachusetts	Senior Analyst

Conducted statistical analyses of information affecting investment program of public, industrial and financial institutions. Interpreted data concerning investment prices, yields, stability and future trends, using daily stock and bond reports, financial periodicals and securities manuals. Performed research and made analyses relative to losses and adverse financial trends. Devised "value line" for utility stocks based on relationship of dividends to bond interest rates. Acted as chief analyst in textile industry.

1945-1967	GEMSTONE SILK, INC. New York, New York	Chief Executive

Complete responsibility for firm, including textile weaving, converting and marketing. Developed processing innovations resulting in substantial cost reductions. Set up data processing system for inventory and production control and sales analysis. Also held positions of Vice President, Plant Manager and Technician. Initiated new testing program for laboratory standards. Developed new materials for use in Navy aircraft.

Education

1970	M.I.T. - Investment Analysis
1969	New York Institute of Finance - Portfolio Management
1965	New York University - Linear Programming

Social Worker   Chronological

SAMUEL H. GREEN
387 PELHAM ROAD
NEW ROCHELLE, NEW YORK 10805
(914) 633-7875

1971-Present   WESTCHESTER COUNTY PAROLE BOARD

Narcotics Parole Officer

Engaged in the rehabilitation of an average caseload
of 40 certified addicts. Developed individualized
programs for each client, according to need. This
involved one-on-one counseling as well as frequent
contact with client's family, incorporating them
into treatment plan.

Created jobs for clients through contact with
community agencies, such as: Operation Upgrade,
and Cellblock Theatre. Provided training in
basic job skills, as well as additional education
through local community programs such as: Operation
Comeback and Office of Vocational Rehabilitation.

1964-1971   WESTCHESTER COUNTY - DEPARTMENT OF SOCIAL SERVICES

Casework Supervisor/Caseworker

Supervised five caseworkers in two years. Instructed
them in agency procedures and casework techniques.
Responsible for managing 300 active cases in the
unit. Maintained controls for numerous required
reports. Created time management system for employees to organize their work for maximum pro-
ductivity.

Provided needed services as a caseworker for families
seeking public assistance. Counseled clients indivi-
dually, gearing the goal to fit each need. Set up
special services such as homemakers for the aged and
blind. Implemented plans such as employment, basic
education and nursing homes. Maintained accurate and
complete records on each client. Achieved highest
record in casework unit in one year of clients' removal
from public assistance roles.

1964   B.B.A.   St. John's University

Used chronological format, as he's staying in the same career area.

Teacher

JAN LEAH ERMAN
1540 42nd Street
Brooklyn, New York 11218

Targeted

JOB TARGET: ELEMENTARY SCHOOL TEACHER

CAPABILITIES:

   *Prepare outlines for daily and monthly course of
    study.
   *Lecture and demonstrate with audiovisual teaching
    aids.
   *Prepare, administer and correct tests.
   *Maintain order and discipline in large and small
    classes.
   *Counsel and direct children with learning difficulties.
   *Counsel parents and direct them into remedial action for
    specific cognitive or emotional problems of children.
   *Train and develop children in verbal self-expression.

ACHIEVEMENTS:

   *Trained two learning disabled children to achieve
    full integration in public school class within two
    weeks.
   *Tutored six "underachievers" in remedial reading;
    all six finished in upper 20% of class by end of year.
   *Developed new system for reporting reading comprehension
    analyses now used in school system city-wide.
    Introduced audiovisual techniques for math learning
    into Grade 2 with much success.
   *Cited as Teacher of the Year in school of 800 in 1977.

WORK HISTORY:

1972 - Present   Yeshiva Havram Secular Division - Brooklyn, New York
                  Fifth & Sixth Grades

1971   Dowd Communications   Production Assistant

EDUCATION:

1975   M.S. in Education   New York University
                  Emphasis on Reading in Elementary Schools

1971   B.A. in Sociology   Brooklyn, New York
                  Minor in Elementary Education

Travel Agent   Chronological with Functional Emphasis

ELLEN T. LONDOFF
450 Fort Washington Avenue
New York, New York 10033
(212) 668-3470

WORK EXPERIENCE

LEISURE TRAVEL SALES, INC.
15 East 40th Street
New York, New York

1975-Present

Sales/Marketing: Developed wholesale travel department within this
company. Focused on individual and group travel programs for executive
level, employees, groups, civic, and fraternal organizations. Designed
incentive programs for sales force within several companies.

Advertising: Evaluated profitability of advertising strategy. Responsible
for selecting best vehicles for copy and promotion. Utilized demographical
information and readership data of trade publications and journals for
determining advertising campaign. Personally wrote advertising copy for
major ads.

Research: Examined which specific facilities and destinations would
best service each group's style, budget, and conference needs. Surveyed
industries, and developed individual presentations for conference planning.

Budgeting: Planned budgets for each program. Negotiated hotel contracts.
Costed out internal operational costs (reservations, documentation,
ticketing, itinerary planning). Budgeted out advertising expenditures
from copywriting to final printing and placement stages. In first year
of program reduced operational costs by 20%.

1971-1975

BIGGER MAN APPAREL, INC.
Orange, Connecticut

Customer Service Representative.
Responsible for all manufacturing sources meeting delivery deadline
obligations. Duties included merchandising, pricing, buying, and
general sales. Worked on all phases of company advertising.

EDUCATION

ADELPHI UNIVERSITY, Garden City, New York   B.A.   Liberal Arts

SAMPLE RESUME PARAGRAPHS

On the following pages we have included sample paragraphs relating to occupational titles not fully covered in the sample resumes themselves. Use them as needed in creating your own resume.

ACCOUNT EXECUTIVE

Plan, coordinate, and direct advertising campaign for clients of advertising agency. Confer with client to determine advertising requirements and budgetary limitations, utilizing knowledge of product or service to be advertised, media capabilities, and audience characteristics.

Confer with agency artists, copywriters, photographers, and other media-production specialists to select media to be used and to estimate costs. Submit proposed program and estimated budget to client for approval.

Coordinate activities of workers engaged in marketing research, writing copy, laying out artwork, purchasing media time and space, developing special displays and promotional items, and perform other media-production activities, in order to carry out approved campaign.

ACCOUNTS PAYABLE/RECEIVABLE CLERK

Perform any combination of routine calculating, posting, and verifying duties to obtain primary financial data for use in maintaining accounting records. Post details of business transactions, such as allotments, disbursements, deductions from payrolls, pay and expense vouchers, remittances paid and due, checks, and claims.

Total accounts, using adding machine. Compute and record interest charges, refunds, cost of lost or damaged goods, freight or express charges, rentals, and similar items. Type vouchers, invoices, account statements, payrolls, periodic reports, and other records. Reconcile bank statements.

ACTIVITIES PLANNER—COLLEGE

Provide motivation and successful sales targeting for a team of eight assistant box office managers. Manage ticket sales by coordinating mini-box offices to open in time segments so that tickets are available sixteen hours per day. Scheduled over 150 sports events during junior and senior years. Produced largest sellout for the Big Game Dance in the history of the school.

ADMINISTRATIVE ASSISTANT

Aid executive in staff capacity by coordinating office services, such as personnel, budget preparation and control, housekeeping, records control, and special management studies. Study management methods in order to improve work flow, simplify reporting procedures, or implement cost reductions. Analyze unit operating practices, such as record-keeping systems, forms control, office layout, suggestion systems, personnel and budgetary requirements.

Analyze jobs to delimit position responsibilities for use in wage-and-salary adjustments, promotions, and evaluation of work flow. Study methods of improving work measurements or performance standards. Coordinate collection and preparation of operating reports, such as time-and-attendance records, terminations, new hires, transfers, budget expenditures, and statistical records of performance data.

Prepare reports including conclusions

and recommendations for solution of administrative problems. Issue and interpret operating policies. Review and answer correspondence.

ADVERTISING CLERK

Measure and draw outlines of advertising space on dummy newspaper copy and compile and record identifying data on dummy copy and other work sheets used as guides for production workers. Compute total inches of advertising and news copy for next day's edition, using adding machine, and read chart to determine required number of newspaper pages.

Measure and draw outlines of advertisements in sizes specified onto dummy copy sheets, using pencil and ruler and arranging advertisements on each sheet so that competitive ones do not appear on same page and balance is attained. Record name of advertiser and dimensions of advertisement within ruled outlines and date and page number on each sheet.

Extract data from dummy copy and other sources and record onto lineage breakdown sheets (production work sheets). Deliver dummy copy and lineage breakdown sheets to designated production and administrative personnel for review and use.

ART DIRECTOR

Formulate concepts and supervise workers engaged in executing layout designs for artwork and copy to be presented by visual communications media, such as magazines, books, newspapers, television posters, and packaging. Review illustrative material and confer with client or individual responsible for presentation regarding budget, background information, objectives, presentation approaches, style techniques, and related production factors.

Formulate basic layout and design concept, and conduct research to select and secure suitable illustrative material, or conceive and assign production of material and detail to artists and photographers. Assign and direct staff members to develop design concepts into art layouts and prepare layouts for printing. Review, approve, and present final layouts to client or department head for approval.

AUDITOR

Examine and analyze accounting records for establishment and prepare reports concerning its financial status and operating procedures. Review data regarding material assets, net worth, liabilities, capital stock, surplus, income, and expenditures. Inspect items in books of original entry to determine if proper procedure in recording transactions was followed.

Count cash on hand, inspect notes receivable and payable, negotiable securities, and canceled checks. Verify journal and ledger entries of cash and check payments, purchases, expenses, and trial balances by examining and authenticating inventory items. Report to management concerning scope of audit, financial conditions found, and source and application of funds.

CERTIFIED PUBLIC ACCOUNTANT

Direct and coordinate activities of workers engaged in general accounting, or apply principles of accounting to devise and implement system for general accounting. Direct and coordinate activities or workers engaged in keeping accounts and records, or performing such bookkeeping activities as recording disbursements, expenses, and tax payments.

Prepare individual, division, or consolidated balance sheets to reflect company's assets, liabilities, and capital. Prepare profit and loss statements for specified accounting period. Audit contracts, orders, and vouchers, and prepare reports to substantiate individual transactions prior to settlement. Represent company before government agencies upon certification by agency involved.

CLERK—CIVIL SERVICE

Keep records of selection and assignment of personnel in office that recruits workers from civil service register. Mail announcements of examinations and blank application forms in response to requests. Perform reception duties and answer questions about examinations, eligibility, salaries, benefits, and other pertinent information. Issue application forms to applicants at counter.

Review applications for completeness, accuracy, and eligibility requirements. File application forms, test papers, and records. Review examination ratings and place names of eligible applicants of appointment. Post results of interviews on file cards. Request references from present or past employers concerning applicants. Type reports and forms.

COMMUNICATIONS CONSULTANT

Contact residential, commercial, and industrial telephone company subscribers to ascertain communication problems and needs and promote use of telephone services, utilizing knowledge of marketing conditions, contracts, sales methods, and communications services and equipment.

Discuss communication services, such as telephone, tele-typewriter, or telex, with subscriber representative to inform representative of services available, and obtain information, such as size of physical plant, range of desired communication and type of equipment or service desired.

Consult with other workers regarding communication needs of subscriber to obtain information, such as availability and cost of services or equipment requested. Analyze information obtained to determine practicability of subscriber request and advise subscriber representative on selection and utilization of services. Prepare sales contracts. Review subscriber accounts to determine and evaluate utilization of communication services.

COMMUNITY DEVELOPER

Develop recreational, physical, and cultural programs for senior citizen group. Organize current-event discussion groups, conduct consumer problem surveys, and perform similar activities to stimulate interest in civic responsibility. Help senior citizens use community services available. Provide support to families of senior citizens.

COUNSELING DIRECTOR

Direct personnel engaged in providing educational and vocational guidance for students and graduates. Assign and evaluate work of personnel. Conduct in-service training program for professional staff. Coordinate counseling bureau with school and community services. Analyze counseling and guidance procedures and techniques to improve quality of service.

Counsel individuals and groups relative to personal and social problems, and educational and vocational objectives. Address community groups and faculty members to interpret counseling service. Supervise maintenance of occupational library for use by counseling personnel. Direct activities of testing and occupational service center.

DENTAL ASSISTANT

Assist dentist engaged in diagnostic, operative, surgical, periodontal, preventive, orthodontic, removal and fixed prosthodontic, endodontic, and pedodontic procedures during examination and treatment of patients. Provide diagnostic aids including exposing radiographs, taking and recording medical and dental histories, recording vital signs, making preliminary impressions for study casts, and making occlusal registrations for mounting study casts.

Perform clinical supportive functions, including preparing and dismissing patients, sterilizing and disinfecting instruments and equipment, providing postoperative instructions prescribed by the dentist and preparing tray setups for dental procedures. Assist dentist in management of medical and dental emergencies. Assist in maintaining patient treatment records and maintaining operatory equipment and instruments. Perform laboratory procedures.

DRAFTER

Prepare clear, complete, and accurate working plans and detail drawings from rough or detailed sketches or notes for engineering or manufacturing purposes, according to specified dimensions. Make final sketch of proposed drawing, checking dimension of parts, materials to be used, relation of one part to another, and relations of various parts to whole structure or project. Make adjustments and changes necessary or desired. Ink in lines and letters on pencil drawings as required. Exercise manual skill in manipulation of triangle, T-square, and other drafting tools. Draw charts for representation of statistical data. Draw finished designs from sketches. Utilize knowledge of various machines, engineering practices, mathematics, building materials, and other physical sciences to complete drawings.

EDITORIAL ASSISTANT

Prepare written material for publication. Read copy to detect errors in spelling, punctuation, and syntax. Verify facts, dates, and statistics, using standard reference sources. Rewrite or modify copy to conform to publisher's style and editorial policy and mark copy for typesetter, using standard symbols to indicate how type should be set.

Read galley and pageproofs to detect errors and indicate corrections, using standard proofreading symbols. Confer with authors regarding changes made to manuscript. Select and crop photographs and illustrative materials to conform to space and subject matter requirements.

EDUCATIONAL THERAPIST

Teach elementary and secondary school subjects to educationally handicapped students with neurological or emotional disabilities in schools, institutions, or other specialized facilities. Plan curriculum and prepare lessons and other instructional materials to meet individual needs of students, considering factors, such as physical, emotional, and educational levels of development. Instruct students in specific subject areas, such as English, mathematics, and geography.

Observe students for signs of disruptive

behavior, such as violence, outbursts of temper, and episodes of destructiveness. Counsel students with regard to disruptive behavior, utilizing variety of therapeutic methods. Confer with other staff members to plan programs designed to promote educational, physical, and social development of students.

FASHION COORDINATOR

Promote new fashions and coordinate promotional activities, such as fashion shows, to induce consumer acceptance. Study fashion and trade journals, travel to garment centers, attend fashion shows, and visit manufacturers and merchandise markets to obtain information on fashion trends. Consult with buying personnel to gain advice regarding types of fashions store will purchase and feature for season. Advise publicity and display departments of merchandise to be publicized.

Select garments and accessories to be shown at fashion shows. Provide information on current fashions, style trends, and use of accessories. Contract with models, musicians, caterers, and other personnel to manage staging of shows.

FUND RAISER

Contact individuals and firms by telephone, in person, or by mail to solicit funds for charities or other causes. Take pledges for amount to be contributed or accept immediate cash payments. Sell emblems or other tokens of organization represented.

GUIDANCE DIRECTOR

Organize, administer, and coordinate guidance program in public school system. Formulate guidance policies and procedures. Plan and conduct in-service training program for guidance workers and selected teachers. Plan and supervise testing program in school system and devise and direct use of records, reports, and other material essential to program.

Supervise school placement service. Establish and supervise maintenance of occupational libraries in schools. Coordinate guidance activities with community agencies and other areas of school system. Conduct or supervise research studies to evaluate effectiveness of guidance program.

HEALTH SERVICES—COLLEGE

Assist nurses and receptionists in university clinic. Greet incoming students and take basic medical histories. Handle phone requests for appointments. Type blood donor cards and other necessary medical reports. Occasionally counsel students in distress regarding minor injuries, possible pregnancy, emotional traumas over school.

INDUSTRIAL HYGIENIST

Conduct health program in industrial plant or governmental organization to recognize, eliminate, and control occupational health hazards and diseases. Collect samples of dust, gases, vapors, and other potentially toxic materials for analysis. Investigate adequacy of ventilation, exhaust equipment, lighting, and other conditions that may affect employee health, comfort, or efficiency.

LOBBYIST

Contact and confer with members of legislature and other holders of public office to persuade them to support legislation favorable to clients' interests. Study proposed legislation to determine possible effect on interest of clients, who may be a person, specific group, or general public. Confer with legislators and officials to emphasize supposed weaknesses or merits of specific bills to influence passage, defeat, or amendment of measure or introduction of legislation more favorable to clients' interests.

Contact individuals and groups having similar interests in order to encourage them also to contact legislators and present views. Prepare news releases and informational pamphlets and conduct news conferences in order to state clients' views and to inform public of features of proposed legislation considered desirable or undesirable.

MAILROOM SUPERVISOR

Supervise and coordinate activities of clerks who open, sort, and route mail, and prepare outgoing material for mailing. Read letters and determine department or official for whom mail is intended and inform mail clerk of routing. Compute amount of postage required for outgoing mail according to weight and classification. Compute cost of mail permits from postage meter readings. Interview and recommend hiring of mailroom employees. Train new employees. Maintain personnel records.

MANAGEMENT TRAINEE

Perform assigned duties, under close direction of experienced personnel, to gain knowledge and experience required for promotion to management positions. Receive training and perform duties in departments, such as credit, customer relations, accounting, or sales to become familiar with line and staff functions and operations and management viewpoints

and policies that affect each phase of business.

Observe and study techniques and traits of experienced workers in order to acquire knowledge of methods, procedures, and standards required for performance of departmental duties.

MANAGEMENT CONSULTANT

Consult with client to define need or problem, conduct studies and surveys to obtain data, and analyze data to advise on or recommend solution, utilizing knowledge of theory, principles, or technology of specific discipline or field of specialization. Consult with client to ascertain and define need or problem area, and determine scope of investigation required to obtain solution. Conduct study or survey on need or problem to obtain data required for solution.

Analyze data to determine solution, such as installation of alternate methods and procedures, changes in processing methods and practices, modification of machine or equipment, or redesign of products or services. Advise client on alternate methods of solving need or problem, or recommend specific solution.

MANAGER, RETAIL STORE

Manage retail store engaged in selling specific line of merchandise, as groceries, meat, liquor, apparel, jewelry, or furniture; related lines of merchandise, as radios, televisions, and household appliances; or general line of merchandise.

Perform following duties personally or supervise employees performing duties. Plan and prepare work schedules and assign employees to specific duties. Formulate pricing policies on merchandise according to requirements for profitability of store operations. Coordinate sales promotion activities and prepare, or direct workers preparing, merchandise displays and advertising copy.

Supervise employees engaged in, or performing, sales work, taking of inventories, reconciling cash with sales receipts, keeping operating records, or preparing daily record of transactions for accountant. Order merchandise or prepare requisitions to replenish merchandise on hand. Ensure compliance of employees with established security, sales, and record-keeping procedures and practices.

MECHANICAL ENGINEER

Plan and design mechanical or electromechanical products or systems, and direct and coordinate operation and repair activities. Design products or systems, such as instruments, controls, engines, machines, and mechanical, thermal, hydraulic, or heat transfer systems, utilizing and applying knowledge of engineering principles.

MEDICAL RECORD ADMINISTRATOR

Plan, develop, and administer medical record systems for hospital, clinic, health center, or similar facility, to meet standards of accrediting and regulatory agencies. Collect and analyze patient and institutional data. Assist medical staff in evaluating quality of patient care and in developing criteria and methods for such evaluation.

Develop and implement policies and procedures for documenting, storing, and retrieving information, and for processing medical-legal documents, insurance, and correspondence requests, in conformance with federal, state, and local statutes. Develop in-service educational materials and conduct instructional programs for health care personnel. Supervise staff in preparing and analyzing medical documents. Provide consultant services to health care facilities, health data systems, related health organizations, and governmental agencies. Engage in basic and applied research in health care field.

MERCHANDISE MANAGER

Formulate merchandising policies and coordinate merchandising activities in wholesale or retail establishment. Determine markup and markdown percentages necessary to ensure profit, based on estimated budget, profit goals, and average rate of stock turnover. Determine amount of merchandise to be stocked and direct buyers in purchase of supplies for resale. Consult with other personnel to plan sales promotion programs.

PACKAGE DESIGNER

Design containers for products, such as foods, beverages, toiletries, cigarettes, and medicines. Confer with representatives of engineering, marketing, management, and other departments to determine packaging requirements and type of product market. Sketch design of container for specific product, considering factors, such as convenience in handling and storing, distinctiveness for identification by consumer, and simplicity to minimize production costs.

Render design, including exterior markings and labels, using paints and brushes. Typically fabricate model in paper, wood, glass, plastic, or metal, depending on material to be used in package. Make modifications required by approving authority.

PLANT ENGINEER

Direct and coordinate, through engineering and supervisory personnel, activities concerned with design, construction, and maintenance of equipment in accordance with engineering principles and safety regulations. Directly oversee maintenance of plant buildings. Coordinate re-surveys, new designs, and maintenance schedules with operating requirements. Prepare bid sheets and contracts for construction and facilities acquisition. Test newly installed machines and equipment to ensure fulfillment of contract specifications.

PROJECT DIRECTOR

Plan, direct, and coordinate activities of designated project to ensure that aims, goals, or objectives specified for project are accomplished in accordance with prescribed priorities, time limitation, and funding conditions. Review project proposal or plan to ascertain time frame and funding limitations, and to determine methods and procedures for accomplishment of project, staffing requirements, and allotment of funds to various phases of project. Develop staffing plan and establish work plan and schedules for each phase of project in accordance with time limitations and funding.

Recruit or request assignment of personnel according to staffing plan. Confer with staff to outline project plans, designate personnel who will have responsibilities for phases or project, and establish scope of authority. Direct and coordinate activities of project through delegated subordinates and establish budget control system for controlling expenditures. Review project reports on status of each phase and modify schedules as required. Prepare project status reports for management. Confer with project personnel to provide technical advice and to assist in solving problems.

PUBLIC RELATIONS REPRESENTATIVE

Plan and conduct public relations program designed to create and maintain favorable public image for employer or client. Plan and direct development and communication of information designed to keep public informed of employer's programs, accomplishments, or point of view. Arrange for public-relations efforts in order to meet needs, objectives, and policies of individual, special interest group, business concern, nonprofit organization, or governmental agency, serving as in-house staff member or as outside consultant.

Prepare and distribute fact sheets, news releases, photographs, scripts, motion pictures, or tape recordings to media representatives and other persons who may be interested in learning about or publicizing employer's activities or message. Purchase advertising space and time as required. Arrange for and conduct public-contact programs designed to meet employer's objectives, utilize knowledge of changing attitudes and opinions of consumers, client's employees, or other interest groups.

Promote goodwill through such publicity efforts as speeches, exhibits, films, tours, and question/answer sessions. Represent employer during community projects and at public, social, and business gatherings.

RESEARCH NUTRITIONIST

Conduct nutritional research to expand knowledge in one or more phases of dietetics. Plan, organize, and conduct programs in nutrition, foods, and food service systems, evaluating and utilizing appropriate methodology and tools to carry out program. Study and analyze recent scientific discoveries in nutrition for application in current research, for development of tools for future research, and for interpretation to the public. Communicate findings through reports and publications.

RESIDENCE COUNSELOR

Provide individual and group guidance services relative to problems of scholastic, educational, and personal-social nature to dormitory students. Suggest remedial or corrective actions and assist students in making better adjustments and in intelligent planning of life goals. Plan and direct program to orient new students and assist in their integration into campus life. Initiate and conduct group conferences to plan and discuss programs and policies related to assignment of quarters, social and recreational activities, and dormitory living. Supervise dormitory activities. Investigate reports of misconduct and attempts to resolve or eliminate causes of conflict.

SALES MANAGER

Supervise and coordinate activities of workers in one department of a retail store: Assign duties to workers and schedule lunch and break periods, work hours, and vacations. Train workers in store policies, department procedures, and job duties. Assist sales workers in completing difficult sales. Evaluate worker performance and recommend retention, transfer, or dismissal of worker. Listen to customer complaints, examine returned merchandise, and attempt to resolve problems and restore and promote good public relations.

Order merchandise, supplies, and equipment as necessary. Ensure that merchandise is correctly priced and displayed. Prepare sales and inventory reports. Approve checks for payment of merchandise and issue credit or cash refund on returned merchandise. Suggest purchase of merchandise and issue credit or cash refund on returned merchandise. Suggest purchase of merchandise for department. Plan department layout on merchandise or advertising display.

SOCIOLOGIST

Conduct research into development, structure, and behavior of groups of human beings and patterns of culture and social organization which have arisen out of group life in society. Collect and analyze scientific data concerning social phenomena, such as community, associations, social institutions, ethnic minorities, social classes, and social change.

STUDENT AFFAIRS DIRECTOR

Plan and arrange social, cultural, and recreational activities of various student groups, according to university policies and regulations. Meet with student and faculty groups to plan activities. Evaluate programs and suggest modifications. Schedule events to prevent overlapping and coordinate activities with sports and other university programs.

Contact caterers, entertainers, decorators, and others to arrange for scheduled events. Conduct orientation program for new students with other members of faculty and staff. Advise student groups on financial status of and methods for improving their organizations. Promote student participation in social, cultural, and recreational activities.

SYSTEMS ANALYST

Analyze business procedures and problems to refine data and convert it to programmable form for electronic data processing. Confer with personnel of organizational units to ascertain specific output requirements, such as types of breakouts, degree of data summarization, and format for management reports. Study existing data-handling systems to evaluate effectiveness and develop new systems to improve production or work flow as required.

Specify in detail logical and/or mathematical operations to be performed by various equipment units and/or comprehensive computer programs, and operations to be performed by personnel in system. Conduct special studies and investigations pertaining to development of new information systems to meet current and projected needs. Plan and prepare technical reports, memoranda, and instructional manuals relative to the establishment and functioning of complete operational systems.

TABULATING MACHINE OPERATOR

Operate machine that processes data from tabulating cards into printed records. Wire and install tabulating-machine plugboard, or insert prewired control panel, using wrenches and screwdriver. Position stack of cards to be tabulated and start machine. Observe machine for malfunctioning and remove jammed cards. Route processed cards to next work station. Tend machines that perform individual functions, such as sorting, interpreting, reproducing, and collating.

TEACHER'S AIDE

Assist teaching staff of public or private elementary or secondary school by performing any combination of following instructional tasks in classroom. Discuss assigned teaching area with classroom teacher to coordinate instructional efforts. Prepare lesson outline and plan in assigned area and submit it for review. Plan, prepare, and develop various teaching aids, such as bibliographies, charts, and graphs.

MANAGING YOUR JOB CAMPAIGN

THE WORKLIFE REVOLUTION . . . AND YOU

You can make a difference in the quality of your worklife. It's as simple as that. As you expand your understanding of how the job market works, you will uncover a wide range of work possibilities and be more in touch with how to turn these employers on to your capabilities.

It is by understanding the rules of the job game, and igniting your own work consciousness, that you take a leading role in the worklife revolution and join the growing number of people who bring work and life into personal harmony—regardless of the employment rate.

Your Perfect Resume and the Career Discovery Process at the beginning of this book are important steps in the self-directed job campaign. On the following pages are some of the most basic rules and strategies of effective job hunting. For a more detailed discussion of these approaches you are invited to consult the author's recent works in the over-all job finding process:

- *The Hidden Job Market:* New York Times Books
- *28 Days to a Better Job:* Hawthorn Books, New York
- *Guerrilla Tactics in the Job Market:* Bantam Books

and of course any one of many other fine books in the field.

THE HIDDEN JOB MARKET

There is a vast underground market place in which over 75 percent of the job openings rise and fall through the dynamics of word of mouth, personal referral, and good luck. They never show up in the daily classifieds. Some rules for tapping into this career information bank:

- **Don't only pursue advertised positions**—be willing to uncover the name, title, and whole address of anyone in *any* organization related to your job target field, and call that person for information.
- **Make a list of twenty persons**—relatives, family, friends, past employers, professors, authorities in the field, to

whom you could send a personal letter with a few copies of your perfect resume, with the **close** conviction (followed by a phone call) that they could probably forward it to others within your field of interest.

- **Undertake some active research** in directories, trade journals, magazines, and books related to your field, once you have clarity in your job targets. Get the names and addresses of at least twenty potential employers *for each job target* and send them a special cover letter with your super-special resume. If you have some other connection to this person, intimate this.

  Individual contact by name is the most effective way into the interviews—without the competition usually provoked when the job gets advertised. The local telephone book yellow pages are a very good source of names of potential employers. Check under two or three related categories. You can get classified directories from other communities in the United States and Canada by a request to your telephone company business office.

Other research sources to use in uncovering the names and addresses of potential employer contacts should include:

- **Business and product directories**—to find out the best directories for you consult your library or the *Guide to American Directories* (B. Kline & Company, 11 Third Street, Rye, N.Y. 10050).
- **Trade and professional associations**—for names and addresses of the most relevant trade associations, consult National Trade and Professional Associations of the United States and Canada (Columbia Books Inc., Publishers, Washington, D.C.).

- **Back issues of trade publications** in your job target areas—a very valuable source of general and specific information about products, industry trends, and authorities in the field. A comprehensive guide to these journals and other articles and books related to the field can be obtained at the research section of your community or university library.

Organized approach: When you go through the directories and other sources of employer information, have a pack of 3×5 index cards, and list each employer, home address, and phone number on a separate card.

GETTING INTERVIEWS

The purpose of your resume and cover letter is to help you get interviews. There are several proven strategies to assist you in accomplishing this:

- **Call first.** A personal telephone contact with the person with whom you want to have the interview could accelerate the entire process. After you have done your research and obtained the names and addresses and phone numbers of at least twenty-five potential employers in your field, set aside a period of time (preferably early morning) to place calls to the individuals who can make the hiring decisions.
- **Be sure to know the name and title** of the person you want to reach before initiating the call. Also have a rough idea of what you want to say that will be of interest to him or her. (The answer to the question *Why should I hire you?*)
- **Have it all organized in advance** so that you can continue to call for at least

two hours without having exhausted your cards. Then take a couple of hours off to recharge your batteries.

- **Primary objective of call:** To set up an interview directly with the appropriate person.
- **Secondary objective:** To establish personal contact that can be followed up by your resume and cover letter.
- **Resistance:** You will have to slug your way through walls of resistance in this phoning: Your resistance (for fear of rejection) and theirs (for fear that you are going to waste their time). The antidote: keep on calling. A string of turndowns is an expected phenomenon in any productive job campaign. As a matter of fact, the whole process looks like this: No No No No No No No No   *Yes.* The only way through is to create more noes faster. Gets you to the yeses that much sooner.
- **Resume/phone call:** This is a second approach, in which you send out your resume and cover letter first, indicating at the conclusion of your letter that you will be calling to set up the interview. Keep good records of when these letters go out, and call the recipient *five* days from the date you mailed it. This is designed to time your call for approximately the day after the employer's representative received it. *Make these follow-up calls on schedule.*

  Watch out for the tendency to procrastinate on the follow-ups. In either telephonic approach to getting interviews, the measure of success is *action*—watch the resistance and barriers come up, and keep on calling.
- **Be prepared.** Know who the employer is (place, size, employees, branches, brief history). And what they *do:* products, services, markets, competitors, projects, achievements. Know that the way you are prepared is read as a direct demonstration of how you will get your job done. Simple but true. Get and read brochures, trade journals, and annual reports. Ask people in the field, competitors, trade associations, and employers.
- **Get a 3 × 5 index card.** On one side, write down five things you want the employer to know about you. On the other side list five questions you want to ask the employer during the interview. Put this card in your pocket or purse and take it with you to the interview and consult it.
- **Get feedback.** It's all right to ask the employer if you have the skills he or she is looking for. The worst it will be is no. In which case you get to find out why. Correction furthers.
- **Dress like a winner.** It's simple: Let your clothes (hair, weight, make-up, complexion) support your purpose in life. Have your personal presentation demonstrate where you are *aiming for.* Not where you *are.*
- **Be "outrageous."** Break your old image of yourself. Go after what you want with high intention, determination, and willingness to operate in the work world at an entirely new level.
- **Role play.** Have a colleague or companion play employer and ask you the five following role-play questions:

  1. What are your strongest abilities?
  2. How do your skills relate to our needs?
  3. What are you looking for in a job?
  4. What would you like to know about us?
  5. Why should we hire you?

- **Critique yourself.** And have your partner do the same.

MAKE MORE MONEY

Please realize that the name of the game is *satisfaction,* not money—work success is having a job that works for you, that lets you be yourself in the work you do. There is very little inherent satisfaction in the money you make—most of us keep our salary hopes two jumps ahead of our earnings throughout our careers regardless of how much we make.

But make more money anyway. The more you make, the bigger the jobs you get, and the more fun the game is. Briefly, here's how:

• Remember that the cardinal economic principle is this: *money follows value.* The way you make more money is to create more value, and stay with value creation until the results are so good that it is impossible not to compensate you out of the value you create.

Three specific salary negotiating techniques:

1. Always let the employer name the salary figure first. Employers tend to cite higher figures than candidates. Interesting, and true. Don't answer the question "What's the minimum salary you would accept?" Tell him you're not looking for the minimum and that you will be taking a number of interviews, expect several offers, and will take the one that offers you the best combination of challenge and compensation. Smile nicely as you say it.

2. Whenever a range is named, verbalize the top of the range.

Employer: The range is $13,000 to $16,000 per year.

You: $16,000 sounds in the right ball park right now.

3. Never accept an offer when it's given. Tell the person who makes it that you appreciate the opportunity, know you can make a contribution, and need to consider it for ten days or so. This shifts the game immediately into your hand as the employer starts to wonder what else you have been offered. Sometimes offers are increased 10 to 20 percent within a week.

And, again, be outrageous, know that it is you who actually let the employer know what you're worth. Be willing to turn down or be turned down if salary isn't right. Go for it!

A LAST WORD. Thank you for staying with us until the end—for us. A beginning for you, we hope, of a new clarity and assertiveness in your resume, and your career search.

Please know that our purpose is strongly behind you, and our support, too. This is a time for all of us to recognize the abundance of opportunity—not necessarily job slots, but true opportunity—for us to make a self-directed contribution to the world in work terms, to get the job done in a way that produces satisfaction and aliveness for ourselves, and value for others.

All of us who assisted in this book send you our love and best wishes for a glorious worklife.